National Defense Research Institute

A Strategic Governance Review

for

Multi-organizational Systems of Education, Training, and Professional Development

Glenn A. Daley ◆ Dina G. Levy ◆ Tessa Kaganoff
Catherine A. Augustine ◆ Roger Benjamin
Tora K. Bikson ◆ Susan M. Gates ◆ Joy S. Moini

RAND

Prepared for the
Office of the Secretary of Defense

The research described in this report was sponsored by the Office of the Secretary of Defense (OSD). The research was conducted in RAND's National Defense Research Institute, a federally funded research and development center supported by the OSD, the Joint Staff, the unified commands, and the defense agencies under Contract DASW01-01-C-0004.

Library of Congress Cataloging-in-Publication Data

A strategic governance review for multi-organizational systems of education, training, and professional development / Glenn A. Daley ... [et al.].
   p. cm.
   "MR-1560."
   Includes bibliographical references.
   ISBN 0-8330-3267-4
   1. United States. Dept. of Defense—Reorganization. 2. United States. Dept. of Defense—Employees—Training of. 3. United States. Dept. of Defense—Employees—Education (Higher) 4. United States. Dept. of Defense—Employees—Continuing education. I. Daley, Glenn A., 1953–

UB193 .S75 2003
355.6'1—dc21

2002031848

Published 2003 by RAND
1700 Main Street, P.O. Box 2138, Santa Monica, CA 90407-2138
1200 South Hayes Street, Arlington, VA 22202-5050
201 North Craig Street, Suite 202, Pittsburgh, PA 15213-1516
RAND URL: http://www.rand.org/
To order RAND documents or to obtain additional information, contact Distribution Services: Telephone: (310) 451-7002; Fax: (310) 451-6915; Email: order@rand.org

As one of the largest employers in the country, the Department of Defense (DoD) seeks to maintain a high-quality civilian workforce in the face of shifting organizational priorities as well as technological and social changes. Like most employers, DoD offers its employees opportunities for education, training, and professional development (ET&D) through both DoD and non-DoD providers. This network of ET&D providers and users constitutes a multi-organizational, multi-stakeholder system that is at present loosely coordinated and incompletely understood. Because of the division of financial responsibility, command authority, and workforce planning within DoD, the effectiveness of the system depends on its capacity for governance of the organizations that provide the ET&D needed.

At the request of the DoD Office of the Chancellor for Education and Professional Development, RAND undertook a study to develop tools for describing and evaluating external governance in such a multi-organizational system of ET&D. This report describes an approach for accomplishing those aims. The approach described here consists of two major tasks: a *structural analysis* that maps governance arrangements and an *implementation audit* that assesses effectiveness based on operational evidence. The framework and taxonomy presented here were developed based on reviews of relevant literature and limited mapping exercises, but not through field audits or assessment exercises with organizations. We recommend pilot testing of the approach on a limited scale before systemwide implementation.

This report is one of a series of reports on ET&D prepared for the Chancellor's office by RAND. A companion document (Augustine et al., 2002) develops an approach for assessing interorganizational influence in complex, nonhierarchical systems. Earlier reports address strategic planning approaches for organizations such as the Chancellor's office (Levy et al., 2001a) and approaches for ensuring quality and productivity in systems of education (Gates et al., 2001).

This report focuses on the DoD challenge but also attempts to address issues in common with other large systems of ET&D. As a result, it may be of interest to higher education administrators and managers of corporate ET&D systems.

This research was conducted for the U.S. Department of Defense Office of the Chancellor for Education and Professional Development within the Forces and Resources Policy Center of RAND's National Defense Research Institute, a federally funded research and development center sponsored by the Office of the Secretary of Defense, the Joint Staff, the unified commands, and the defense agencies.

CONTENTS

Preface iii

Figures ix

Summary xi

Acknowledgments xix

Acronyms xxi

Chapter One
    INTRODUCTION 1
    Objective 1
    Background 2
    The Value of Reviewing External Governance 3
    Approach 6
        Components of the Strategic Governance Review 6
        Development of the Review 8
    Organization of the Report 10

Chapter Two
    THE DOD CHALLENGE 11
    DoD Civilian Education, Training, and Development 12
    Relevant Characteristics of the System 14
        Heterogeneity 14
        Independent Evolution 15
        Hybrid Form 15
    The Chancellor's Office 16

Chapter Three
  THE STRUCTURAL ANALYSIS OF EXTERNAL
  GOVERNANCE   19
  A Taxonomy   19
    External Governance   20
    Providers   21
    Stakeholders   22
    Systems   22
    Special Stakeholder Types   23
    Stakeholder Influence   28
    Governance Functions   29
    Domains   31
  Mapping Governance Arrangements   32
    Sources of Information   33
    Cataloging Arrangements   34
    Drawing a Governance Map   35
    Mapping Indirect Governance Relationships   36
    Additional Lessons from the Mapping Exercise   40
  Aligning Governance Arrangements   41

Chapter Four
  THE IMPLEMENTATION AUDIT OF EXTERNAL
  GOVERNANCE   49
  Overview   49
    Defining the Assessment of Governance Effectiveness . .   51
  Planning the Audit   53
    The Purpose of the Audit   54
    The Scope of the Audit   55
    Selecting Criteria   56
    Determining Who Will Conduct the Audit   58
    Gathering Operational Information   59
  Assessing the Effectiveness of External Governance   60
    Criterion 1. There Is Evidence that System Outcomes
      Are Being Defined, Measured, and Evaluated Relative
      to Goals   61
    Criterion 2. There Is Evidence that Providers,
      Intermediaries, and Key Stakeholders Are
      Communicating Frequently and Transparently   62
    Criterion 3. There Is Evidence that Providers and
      Intermediaries Are Responsive to Key Stakeholder
      Guidance   63

Criterion 4. There Is Evidence that Key Stakeholders
  Are Being Satisfied   65
Reporting and Follow-Up   66
  Responding to Preliminary Findings   67
  Generating Recommendations and Conclusions   67
  Implementation and Evaluation   67
  Reviewing the Audit   68
Chapter Five
  RECOMMENDATIONS AND CONCLUSIONS   69
Bibliography   73

FIGURES

1.1. A Strategic Review of External Governance   6
3.1. A Multi-Organizational System of ET&D 23
3.2. Examples of Stakeholders, Governance Functions,
     and Domains of ET&D 32
3.3. External Governance Map for a Single Provider—
     Direct Links 37
3.4. External Governance Map for a Single Provider —with
     Indirect Links and System Included 38

INTRODUCTION AND BACKGROUND

The Department of Defense (DoD) provides its civilian employees with numerous opportunities for education, training, and professional development (ET&D). For this purpose, it operates, sponsors, or contracts with various providers of ET&D ranging from line agencies that offer short courses to major institutions of higher education. Thus, the provision of ET&D forms a loose and complex multi-organizational network of providers, employers, sponsors, and other stakeholders, including licensing boards, boards of visitors and advisors, and accrediting bodies. We call the influencing functions assumed by those stakeholders *external governance.*

Systems can be governed through formal and informal mechanisms. Moreover, governance may be executed through a wide range of entities, including those within and outside the system. In the case of the DoD system of ET&D, governance cuts across the boundaries of organizations with missions other than ET&D and operates through multiple channels of authority and influence. The fulfillment of the mission and purpose of such a system may depend on the ability of system leaders to control, coordinate, or influence (i.e., govern) the elements of the system that create final outputs, namely, the providers of ET&D.

Oversight of the quality and productivity of ET&D activities was made a focus of policy in 1998, when the DoD Office of the Chancellor for Education and Professional Development was established. The Chancellor's office was tasked with serving as the primary advocate for the academic quality and cost-effectiveness of ET&D for DoD civilians, although it was given relatively little direct authority over the providers, and governance remains decentralized and complicated. In pursuit of its mission, the Chancellor's office seeks to identify and help eliminate governance obstacles to the establishment and achievement of system goals.

OBJECTIVE AND APPROACH

The aim of this work is to provide the Chancellor's office with tools that enable the description and evaluation of the external governance of ET&D providers serving DoD civilians. Accordingly, the report describes an approach for conducting a *strategic governance review* consisting of two types of examination: a *structural analysis* and an *implementation audit*. The primary goal of a structural analysis is to describe existing governance arrangements. The analysis includes a mapping task in which providers and stakeholders, their functions and goals, and the relationships among them are identified. It proceeds by explicitly linking system-level goals with governance arrangements and by searching for gaps and overlaps in the coverage of critical goals. The primary goal of an implementation audit, on the other hand, is to assess governance. It involves checking actual governance practices and evaluating them against effectiveness criteria. This report does not present the results of any such analyses; it proposes an approach to conducting them that may be used by system-level authorities in their own studies of governance within their particular contexts.

THE STRUCTURAL ANALYSIS OF EXTERNAL GOVERNANCE

The structural analysis is the first task in conducting a strategic governance review. Its goal is to identify the structure of governance within a system. It is supported by a taxonomy that establishes labels for the various elements of external governance, including the entities involved in governance, the functions of governance, and the domains of ET&D subject to governance.

A Taxonomy

We define *external governance* as a set of relationships between providers of ET&D and the stakeholders that exert influence over the nature, quality, and cost-effectiveness of the education offered. Because we have defined governance in terms of influence, and not formal authority, we distinguish among formal (i.e., documented or explicit) governance arrangements, informal (i.e., not formally documented, but implicit) governance arrangements, and actual influence relationships, which may or may not coincide with formal or informal arrangements.

Providers are the institutions, programs, and courses of instruction that deliver ET&D to students. *Stakeholders* are the persons or organizations external to providers that have interests in the provision of ET&D and that may seek to influence providers on behalf of such interests. *Systems* consist of sets of related providers and the stakeholders that influence them or have interests in the ET&D they provide.

In mapping stakeholders, it helps to consider certain types that might be overlooked without special emphasis. These are not categories, but roles that are often overlapping. We characterize these types of stakeholders as demand-side stakeholders, system-level stakeholders, peripheral stakeholders, and intermediaries, defined as follows:

- *Demand-side stakeholder.* An individual who receives or might receive ET&D from providers, and the individual's actual and potential employers or other sponsors. In workforce ET&D, where students are employees, and employers authorize and sponsor their training, the employers constitute the key demand-side stakeholder group.

- *System-level stakeholder.* A person or organization that is charged with responsibility for the overall mission of a system. This type of stakeholder is emphasized because of the mission-oriented nature of DoD, so that the governance analysis does not become simply a balancing of all stakeholder interests regardless of the system mission.

- *Peripheral stakeholder.* A person or organization that has goals, interests, or concerns at stake in the provision of ET&D other than the primary mission of the system, and that does not directly benefit from ET&D as an employer of the trained workforce.

- *Intermediary.* A person or organization that exercises influence over a provider or system on behalf of other stakeholders, rather than primarily in pursuit of its own goals, concerns, or interests.

Functions are the tasks that stakeholders carry out with respect to other persons or organizations in the ET&D system. We classify functions into four broad categories: (1) command and control; (2) resource provision; (3) coordination and/or communication; and (4) evaluation, research, planning, advising, and/or advocacy.

Domains are the areas of ET&D provision that stakeholders seek to influence. Examples of domains include mission, structure, operations, services, curriculum, personnel, and admissions.

Mapping Governance Arrangements

Mapping external governance arrangements involves answering six questions:

1. Who are the providers in the ET&D system under review?

2. What stakeholders are directly involved in external governance for these providers?

3. What governance functions are performed by each of these stakeholders?

4. Over what domains do these stakeholders exercise or seek influence?

5. What other stakeholders do intermediaries represent?

6. What interactions among stakeholders are relevant to the governance of ET&D?

The answers to the first four questions determine the scope of the structural analysis and permit the mapping of direct relationships between stakeholders and providers of ET&D. Answering the final two questions introduces another order of complexity into the mapping task, because it requires identification of indirect relationships between governance stakeholders and ET&D providers.

Aligning Governance Arrangements

After governance arrangements are mapped, system-level planners can evaluate the extent to which those arrangements cover key stakeholder goals. Such a task requires the identification of key stakeholders and their goals and matches the goals with governance functions.

Identification of key stakeholders requires an exercise of judgment based on the purpose of the review. Identification of key goals can be achieved by studying the nature and mission of organizations both as expressed in official documents and through interviews with leaders and administrators. We suggest four broad categories as a guide for identifying goals for a system of ET&D: (1) providing/obtaining a skilled workforce (effectiveness or quality), (2) making efficient use of resources (cost-effectiveness or productivity), (3) maintaining a high quality of life for workers (i.e., students), and (4) maintaining equity or fairness. These categories are not intended to be exhaustive or mutually exclusive. After key stakeholders and their goals are identified, the following questions can be asked: first, who is acting on behalf of the stakeholders to protect the achievement of the goals, and second, what governance functions are being performed regarding the goals?

Once these basic questions are answered, the analysis begins to include questions that will be more directly useful in assessing the effectiveness of governance. What are the obstacles or threats to the achievement of the key goals? Are there significant gaps and/or overlaps in the coverage of key goals and functions?

THE IMPLEMENTATION AUDIT OF EXTERNAL GOVERNANCE

The goal of the implementation audit is to assess the effectiveness of governance practice. It requires detailed evidence from organizations in the system demonstrating how governance works in practice. As a result, it requires more time, staff effort, and multi-organizational participation than does a structural analysis. An implementation audit is carried out to address concerns about governance capabilities and outcomes, and it must rest on a preliminary understanding of the system as provided by a structural analysis.

Planning the Audit

A successful and efficient audit requires careful planning. Decisions must be made about the purpose and scope of the audit, who is to conduct the audit, and how information is to be gathered. Perhaps the most important step in the planning process is the specification of criteria for effectiveness. Criteria should be measurement based, mission driven, and outcome oriented. Measurement-based criteria enable objective assessment. Mission-driven criteria direct the assessment toward the purpose of the system. Outcome-oriented criteria focus on results. In cases where outcomes cannot be observed, process-oriented criteria can be substituted, but evidence should be presented linking the process to the outcomes it is intended to generate.

The audit involves gathering evidence as to how well the system fulfills the preset effectiveness criteria. Auditors obtain evidence about the day-to-day implementation of governance relationships among entities and then consider the weight of the evidence relative to each criterion. Specific types of evidence should be named in the governance audit plan and requested from entities subject to the audit. Site visits and interviews can be used to supplement the documentary evidence.

Assessing the Effectiveness of External Governance

We suggest four criteria for assessing how well existing arrangements and relationships govern the achievement of the system's mission and the satisfaction of stakeholder goals. Accordingly, these criteria require evidence relating specifically to governance performance and not ultimate system performance.

1. There is evidence that system outcomes are being measured and evaluated relative to goals. Effective governance requires that outcomes be measured on an ongoing basis and evaluated relative to the mission, vision, and goals established for the system by system-level stakeholders.

2. There is evidence that providers, intermediaries, and key stakeholders are communicating frequently and transparently. Frequent and transparent two-way communication informs providers of stakeholders' expectations and makes stakeholders aware of the efforts of providers and the constraints they face in meeting expectations.

3. There is evidence that providers and intermediaries are responsive to key stakeholder guidance. To address this criterion, auditors can seek evidence that external governing entities have succeeded in influencing the provision of ET&D within the domain of interest.

4. There is evidence that key stakeholders are being satisfied. Governance success can be measured indirectly by assessing stakeholders' satisfaction with their own goal outcomes. Evidence of stakeholder satisfaction is a positive sign, but considered alone, it does not demonstrate effective governance. On the other hand, stakeholder dissatisfaction constitutes strong evidence that governance is ineffective.

Reporting and Follow-Up

After the assessment has been performed, the organizations involved in the audit should be informed of preliminary findings and given an opportunity to respond. Observations and recommendations should be documented and disseminated, and the audit itself should be reviewed for lessons that will make future audits more efficient and effective.

RECOMMENDATIONS AND CONCLUSIONS

Based on this study, we recommend the following for the Chancellor's office, the DoD system of ET&D, and others who might make use of the tools presented here:

- *Advocate and facilitate system-level and demand-side governance by key stakeholders.* If there are system-level stakeholders, there should be a system-level approach to governance. Demand-side stakeholders may lack influence in a system where the provision of ET&D cuts across the boundaries of organizations with missions other than ET&D. Even in decentralized systems, a system-level strategic review of governance can empower key stakeholders to exercise more effective governance in pursuit of their own goals.

- *Encourage key stakeholders to undertake a structural analysis of governance as part of their own strategic planning function.* A system's first structural analysis is likely to yield major benefits, and occasional revisits can help ensure that governance arrangements remain aligned with stakeholder goals.

- *Engage in system-specific development and pilot testing before performing an implementation audit of governance.* Because the model presented in this report has not been formally tested, any audit based on this model should be tailored to the system being audited and should be pilot tested before being performed on a large scale.

- *Perform implementation audits on a case-by-case basis for major subsystems or key stakeholders that have salient problems with responsiveness to governance and effectiveness in achieving goals.* Auditing the implementation of governance can be costly, so it should be done only in response to perceived problems with the governance of subsystems.

- *Establish a center for the development and retention of governance knowledge and evaluation capacity.* The Chancellor's office could serve as such a center for DoD civilian ET&D. It is suitably positioned to perform a system-level structural analysis of governance, and it could support system-level stakeholders who choose to conduct implementation audits.

ACKNOWLEDGMENTS

We thank Chancellor Jerome Smith and Dr. James Raney of the DoD Office of the Chancellor for Education and Professional Development for their support of this work. The work benefited from interactions with Paul Light of the Brookings Institution, Fred Thompson and Debra Ringold of Willamette University, and James Dewar of RAND. Al Robbert, Laura Zakaras, Susan Everingham, and Fred Thompson provided helpful reviews of earlier drafts.

DAU   Defense Acquisition University

DCAA   Defense Contract Audit Agency

DLIFLC   Defense Language Institute Foreign Language Center

DoD   Department of Defense

ET&D   Education, training, and professional development

FAO   Field audit office

HR   Human resources

OMB   Office of Management and Budget

OSD   Office of the Secretary of Defense

USD(AT&L)   Under Secretary of Defense for Acquisition, Technology, and Logistics

Chapter One

INTRODUCTION

OBJECTIVE

The purpose of this report is to provide the Office of the Chancellor for Education and Professional Development in the Department of Defense (DoD) with concepts for clarifying and approaches for evaluating the external governance of education, training, and professional development (ET&D) providers serving DoD.[1] These concepts and approaches are intended as tools that the Chancellor's office may use in its efforts to influence the quality and cost-effectiveness of ET&D within DoD or may recommend to DoD functional sponsors to use in their own efforts to understand and evaluate the responsiveness of the providers that serve them. Although intended primarily for the Chancellor's office and functional sponsors, the

---

[1] *External* governance here means governance from outside of the provider organization, although it is internal to DoD as the overarching system. As discussed in Chapter Three, *Governance* in this report includes not only the traditional command-and-control functions but also resource provision, coordination, communication, and other interorganizational support functions that outside entities may perform in a relationship of influence.

Furthermore, this report focuses on the governance of the specific courses, programs, and institutions that provide the operational elements of ET&D, not on the strategic planning that determines the role of ET&D in the larger DoD system. In previous work, this research team examined strategic planning alternatives for the Chancellor's office (Levy et al., 2001a) and recommended that the Chancellor's office advocate the development of a learning organization approach within DoD (Gates et al., 2001). Both of those reports emphasize that a system-level approach in the DoD context requires interactions among operationally separate organizations, giving rise to the specific concern about external governance that underlies the present report.

tools may also prove useful to the providers themselves as they seek to understand and improve their own governance arrangements.

BACKGROUND

Postsecondary ET&D for DoD civilians involves multiple and varied providers. These include educational institutions such as universities, with their programs and courses, both within and external to DoD. Providers also include programs and courses carried out within organizations that are not primarily educational institutions, again both inside and outside of DoD.

These providers serve employees from multiple and varied organizational employers under the broad DoD umbrella. As expected, there are also multiple and varied entities that have a stake in influencing how providers operate. The term *sponsor* is used in DoD to identify the primary authorities over providers of ET&D (Levy et al., 2001a). There are four types of sponsors: those with direct command authority, those providing funds and other resources, those with an interest in curriculum content based on workforce ET&D requirements, and those that establish system-level policy. These roles often overlap, so that a single office within DoD may perform more than one type of sponsorship or may sponsor multiple providers. In addition to sponsors, there are various other organizations involved in governance, such as boards of advisors or visitors, accrediting agencies, and state licensing authorities.

The diversity of this system presents a challenge to the Office of the Secretary of Defense (OSD) in making sure the ET&D needs of the DoD workforce are met effectively and efficiently. As a response to this situation, in 1998 the Office of the Chancellor for Education and Professional Development in the DoD was established. The Chancellor's office was tasked with acting as the principal advocate for the academic quality and cost-effectiveness of ET&D provided to the civilian workforce in the DoD.

In the course of navigating the complex system of ET&D providers and stakeholders and seeking ways to meet its goals of promoting quality and productivity, the Chancellor's office has contracted RAND to conduct several related studies. One of these, a study of strategic and performance planning for the Chancellor's office (Levy et al., 2001a), led to a number of near-term, medium-term, and life-time strategies for the Chancellor's office to pursue. It suggested a medium-term strategy to eliminate governance obstacles, because complex and unclear lines of authority were found to hinder the achievement of system goals. It also found that strategic planning decisions should be made taking into consideration the governance structures available to support implementation. Another report, on assessment as a means of ensuring academic quality and productivity (Gates et al., 2001), found that the degree and nature of authority an assessor has over providers is an important determinant of assessment effectiveness. The present report represents research sponsored by the Chancellor's office partially in response to these previous findings.

THE VALUE OF REVIEWING EXTERNAL GOVERNANCE

This report is based on the assumption that understanding and evaluating the external governance of providers within such a system is a helpful step toward achieving system-level goals.[2] This assumption will not be tested here; it arises from the previous RAND work cited above and from the perception by the Chancellor's office that external governance is a key issue in the effort to advocate quality and cost-effectiveness in the existing system of ET&D. This section provides some rationale for these assumptions.

In an ideal world, with elements of a system perfectly cooperative and/or perfectly accountable within an unambiguous hierarchy, the external governance of organizations within that system would be straightforward. In the real world, though, a complex system such as the DoD is likely to have evolved over time through the accretion of existing organizations with different histories and the occasional creation of new ones to meet changing requirements or circumstances. (Consider the DoD itself, created in 1949 as a conglomerate of departments—two with independent histories of a century and a

---

[2]The term *goals* is used broadly in this report to refer to the ends or aims toward which behavior is or should be directed. In a specific organizational context, these may be conceived of as goals, objectives, a mission, a vision, or other aim-oriented concepts. However, *system-level goals* imply ends derived in principle from an authority external to the system and include the mission and vision of the system.

half and one newly formed as a spinoff.) Such a system may include organizations of different sizes and structures, pursuing different goals, linked in different types of relationships to each other, and accountable to different stakeholders through multiple channels of authority. There may be competition and conflict among providers, stakeholders, and channels of authority. There may be gaps and redundancies in the governance coverage of system-level goals. From the point of view of a system-level authority, the external governance of organizations within the system may be confusing and weak, or opaque and ineffective.

With respect to its core mission and overall environment, a long-lived system will have found a method of governance that works well enough to ensure survival. To be competitive, a business conglomerate must find an appropriate level and style of control over its subsidiaries. The DoD has developed an approach to governance over its component organizations that enables it to continue serving the national security interest and to obtain the necessary resources from the public. However, the core mission of such a system is likely to consist of something larger than the ET&D of its own employees. Traditionally, each subsidiary or component of a multi-organizational system takes responsibility for ET&D as a function in support of its own primary mission.

In today's environment of business competition and the demand for effectiveness and efficiency in public agencies, employee ET&D is increasingly treated as a system-level function.[3] This means that ET&D activities, resources, and providers are shared across the boundaries of component organizations or divisions in an attempt to obtain system-level benefits such as economies of scale, elimination of redundancies, interdivisional sharing of knowledge, and coordination of content with strategic plans. However, such system-level ET&D is no longer the responsibility of line organizations in terms of their own missions, but becomes the mission of providers that may exist within, across, and/or separately from line organizations. A complex system may depend on a multi-channel style of governance

---

[3]See the literature on the learning organization (Senge, 1990) and knowledge management (Wiig, 1997).

to ensure that providers respond to the system's goals of quality and productivity while meeting the operational needs of multiple customer organizations.[4]

Given a strategic decision to conduct ET&D across organizational lines and to advocate system-level goals of quality and productivity in all ET&D, the providers of ET&D need to be responsive to system-level guidance. However, the degree and type of external governance needed varies with the characteristics of the organizations, their goals, and the nature of their working relationships.[5] If the goals of member organizations are well aligned with the goals of the overarching system, without conflict between the core missions of components and system-level ET&D goals, the governance function of command and control may be unnecessary. Even in such a case, there may still be a need for coordination and communication as governance functions. One size does not fit all. The approach outlined in this report is intended to help make governance appropriate to the need for it, as determined on a case-by-case basis; it does not just assume that more is always better.

The review of external governance may provide system-level authorities with information that enables them to improve the design of governance structures and the implementation of governance practices. On the other hand, even if it yields no explicit improvement initiatives, it should provide an understanding of the governance background of many strategic planning and academic assessment decisions. In cases where a system is functioning well and self-governing, the review may provide useful insight into the implicit structures and practices underlying such success.

---

[4]A study of the City University of New York (Gill, 2000) shows that even a system with ET&D as its core mission faces the issue of centralized versus decentralized governance and suggests that different governance functions be performed at different levels to obtain both system-level and unit-level benefits wherever possible.

[5]The literature on transaction cost economics describes the degree and mode of governance as dependent on the characteristics of transactions, including asset specificity and uncertainty (Williamson, 1996). Such an approach could be applied to the DoD ET&D context as another research task outside the scope of this report.

APPROACH

To provide the Chancellor's office and functional sponsors with helpful tools for clarifying and evaluating external governance within the DoD system of civilian ET&D, we developed an exploratory conceptual framework and a taxonomy for thinking and talking about external governance in the DoD context. We then developed two approaches for examining external governance in such a system, one focused on the design of governance structures and the other on the implementation of governance practices.

Components of the Strategic Governance Review

Faced with a scenario of multi-organizational complexity and shared, multi-channel governance, an overseeing authority or stakeholder's natural first step is to undertake some sort of examination or strategic review of external governance within the system, as illustrated in Figure 1.1. This report offers a guide to conducting such a *strategic governance review,* consisting of two distinct types of

RAND*MR1560-1.1*

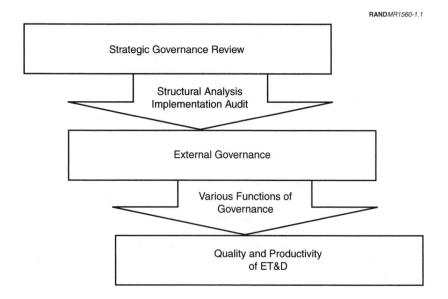

Figure 1.1—A Strategic Review of External Governance

examination, which may be undertaken together or separately: a *structural analysis* and an *implementation audit*. The report does not, however, include results from any actual exercise of these examinations.

- A *structural analysis* represents an attempt to clarify the big picture of external governance within a system. It is intended to help system leaders understand how governance arrangements are organized and specified and to help them plan for organizational and strategic changes. This task involves *mapping* governance: listing the entities involved, their functions and goals, and the normative or expected relationships among them. A visual diagram of these relationships can provide clarity and insight about the complexity of the governance system. Based on such an overview of the system, governance arrangements can be aligned with goals. The structural analysis provides planners an opportunity to make explicit linkages between system-level goals and governance arrangements and to look especially for gaps and overlaps in the coverage of critical goals.

- An *implementation audit*, on the other hand, implies checking actual governance relationships and practices in the field. This task involves *assessing* governance: looking for evidence that the observed processes and outcomes of governance satisfy various chosen criteria relating to effectiveness and efficiency. This type of study should reveal deficiencies and other opportunities for improvement to system-level leaders planning structural or policy changes. It should also provide feedback to the specific organizations involved.

A structural analysis may be done—perhaps should be done—by the overseeing authority as a strategic planning exercise. This task is intended to provide a better understanding of the system from the top down. While the work can be delegated and the results summarized in a report, leaders who engage in the analytical process directly are likely to gain additional insights from the process itself as well as to improve the analysis by contributing their perspectives. Analyzing structure will be an infrequent task, which is unnecessary when the structures of governance are already well understood and adequately cover the system's goals.

On the other hand, an implementation audit may be better done by a relatively independent agency or intermediary. As an evaluation of how well governance works in practice, this task requires detailed field work and an objective perspective that might be inconsistent with delegation to a highly involved component of the system. Repeated auditing of implementation may be warranted to assess the ongoing practice of governance and its effectiveness and efficiency over time.

Development of the Review

To provide the Chancellor's office with the needed concepts and tools, this project consisted of three steps, moving from research in the theory of governance to practical suggestions for evaluating governance, with an intermediate step of supplying a taxonomy for describing external governance arrangements.

The first step was to gather insights from existing literature and synthesize a conceptual framework for understanding external governance in the context of ET&D in the DoD. Much of the literature on governance in higher education and other contexts either focuses on internal governance or assumes a simpler organizational form than the loosely coupled multi-organizational system described here. The literature most relevant and useful to the effort reported here is scattered across various disciplines. The conceptual framework was informed not only by this diverse literature, but also by case studies conducted in the course of prior work for the Chancellor's office (Levy et al., 2001a; Gates et al., 2001).[6]

The second step was to provide a taxonomy and methods for describing external governance arrangements and to refine the initial

---

[6]The cases studied in prior work included state boards of higher education, university systems, accrediting agencies, professional societies, U.S. government departments and agencies other than DoD, professional military ET&D within DoD, and corporate universities and human resources departments. All of the case studies used published information about the organizations being examined; several also included site visits by the research team. However, the primary focus of these case studies was not governance understood broadly, but the specific governance functions of planning and evaluation. As such, the studies provide background knowledge to this framework and taxonomy rather than direct empirical support.

conceptual framework through application and adaptation to DoD. This effort was guided by the criteria that the framework and taxonomy should fit the DoD context, communicate insights relevant to the mission of the Chancellor's office, support a practical approach to reviewing governance, and remain internally consistent.[7] To the extent possible within these criteria, we also sought to avoid straying far from foundations in the scholarly literature and to maintain consistency with current usage in systems of ET&D other than DoD. The result, however, is a heuristic for DoD rather than a universal taxonomy or a general theory of governance.

The structural mapping task described in this report would involve applying this taxonomy to the entities, relationships, and functions of external governance within a given system. Although some examples are provided, this report does not actually carry out such an analysis of governance within DoD.

The third step was to develop a strategy and methods for evaluating the realities of external governance in such a system. Again, we found little existing material directly suited for this purpose in the DoD context but many sources of ideas. Thus, the approach given in this report represents a synthesis, combining the taxonomy of external governance with practical suggestions from the fields of quality auditing, program evaluation, and assessment of higher education.[8]

---

[7]Simultaneously with this work, the team also studied the bases of influence between organizations, as a way of understanding and developing the capacity for governance in multi-organizational systems such as the DoD. That research is reported in Augustine et al. (2002). The governance review described here was influenced by the study of interorganizational influence, and consistency between the two lines of research was a criterion.

[8]It is important to note that assessing external governance in a system of ET&D is not the same as assessing the actual provision of ET&D, as Figure 1.1 illustrates. Gates et al. (2001) describes approaches to ensuring quality and productivity in ET&D activities. The structural analysis in the present report can be seen as an example of the previous report's system level assessment, but with respect to the governance of providers rather than the quality and productivity of ET&D. The implementation audit in the present report can be seen as a variation of the previous report's process audit, but again with respect to governance rather than academic quality and cost-effectiveness.

ORGANIZATION OF THE REPORT

We present an overview of external governance issues facing the DoD system of ET&D in Chapter Two. The reader who is familiar with this context and wants to move quickly into the mapping and auditing sections may skip this material. In Chapter Three we describe the structural analysis of external governance, and in Chapter Four we describe the implementation audit of external governance. In Chapter Five, we offer recommendations for the Chancellor's office, functional sponsors, and others who might consider using these approaches.

Chapter Two

THE DOD CHALLENGE

As discussed in a previous RAND report (Levy et al., 2001a), one of the highest priorities for the DoD is to maintain the quality of its civilian workforce. The importance of this goal can be illustrated in terms of a few key characteristics and trends:

- *Size.* The DoD civilian workforce of some 700,000 employees is one of the largest in the nation.

- *Increasing dependency on civilian labor and outsourcing.* As the uniformed services focus utilization of their military members on war-fighting tasks, more support tasks, along with more responsibility for management, are being shifted to the civilian workforce. Furthermore, many tasks are being contracted to non-DoD providers. While this may reduce the number of DoD employees overall, it shifts the responsibility of the remaining DoD workforce toward higher-level tasks, such as the coordination and supervision of such contracts.

- *High-tech skill requirements.* The DoD depends increasingly on high-tech systems to fulfill its mission, while an era of rapid technological change makes it necessary to upgrade skills continuously.

- *Economic and demographic changes.* With the average age of the population rising and with ethnically and culturally diverse workers realizing gains in employment in the American workforce (Deavers, Lyons, and Hattiangadi, 1999), the civil service and DoD workforce are also changing (Light, 1999; and Levy et al., 2001b). Many of its most experienced personnel are

approaching retirement, creating a need to focus on the development and/or recruitment of qualified replacements. The DoD
workforce problem is, as always (even in times of economic slow-
down), compounded by competition from a generally robust and
highly mobile labor market outside of government.

Like many other employers in both the public and private sectors,
DoD offers its civilian workforce opportunities for ET&D. These opportunities include courses and programs provided by a variety
of institutions and organizational units, including both DoD
activities and external contractors. The goal of maintaining a high-
quality workforce implies achieving a high level of quality and cost-
effectiveness in the system of ET&D that equips workers with the
needed skills and develops them as leaders and professionals.

DOD CIVILIAN EDUCATION, TRAINING, AND DEVELOPMENT

Currently, the OSD sponsors 20 educational provider institutions
within the DoD, more than 100 educational programs both internal
and external to DoD, and numerous courses (Office of the Assistant
Secretary of Defense for Force Management Policy, 1997). In addition, numerous other courses and programs for DoD civilian personnel are available through institutions run, separately from OSD, by
the Departments of the Army, Navy, and Air Force as well as the Joint
Staff. Some of these institutions are accredited, and some offer
academic degree programs. Many of them serve uniformed military
personnel as well as civilians, and many also serve non-DoD students and clients. In some cases, such as programs at major universities, DoD students represent only a small fraction of the total
student body.

While this network of diverse providers serves the needs of civilian
workers throughout DoD, in a more important sense it must serve
the mission of DoD and numerous related institutional needs. Thus,
the ET&D system includes not only the providers and the workers
who participate as students but also the organizational entities that
employ the workers—the many agencies and activities that constitute DoD. Furthermore, DoD itself is a complex network of organizations that provide services to each other as well as to the public, so

numerous organizations with an interest in the skill level of specific segments of the DoD civilian workforce are also interested in ET&D. Thus, there are multiple and varied entities that have a stake in influencing how providers operate.

The term *sponsor* is used in DoD to identify the primary authorities over educational providers.[1] There are four types of sponsor.

- The *command sponsor* is the entity to which the provider institution's head officially reports.

- The *resource sponsor* provides the resources required by the provider (dollars, facilities, and civilian and military personnel authorizations).

- The *functional sponsor* determines and approves curriculum content in light of workforce ET&D requirements in an area of specialization.

- The *policy sponsor* formulates policy and acts as an arbiter when there are conflicts between the other sponsors.

A single entity within DoD may fulfill more than one of these sponsorship roles with respect to a particular institution and may fulfill different roles with respect to different institutions. It is also common for an institution to have more than one functional sponsor.

There are other entities involved in governance. Some institutions have boards of visitors or advisors that provide advice on curriculum or operational issues. Some institutions are accredited by regional, national, and/or specialized accrediting agencies outside the DoD; all DoD provider institutions have been instructed to seek such accreditation. Most providers of training for recognized vocations or providers who serve non-DoD students must also be licensed or chartered by their respective states; again, DoD now expects all its providers to meet such requirements. Any providers outside DoD are accountable to their own boards of trustees and other governing entities.

---

[1]These terms are not always used in authorizing directives, and rarely are all four types identified explicitly. However, even when the terms are not used, their meanings are usually implicit in the responsibilities assigned by the directives.

RELEVANT CHARACTERISTICS OF THE SYSTEM

Such a loosely associated collection of activities and organizations could hardly be called a system except that they all participate in the mission of DoD and answer to the overall authority of the Secretary of Defense. Over time, some major areas of specialization, such as health sciences and acquisition, have evolved into structured subsystems, but many other areas are still relatively uncoordinated. The nature of this system as an aggregate of diverse parts represents a challenge to the OSD in governing how well ET&D is delivered and serves the needs of the DoD workforce.

The governance challenge facing the DoD system of civilian ET&D must be addressed in terms of the characteristics of the system. Some types of system are by nature easily governed, others less so.

Heterogeneity

The DoD system of ET&D consists of large multi-department schools, such as the Uniformed Services University of the Health Sciences; consortia of schools and programs, such as the Defense Acquisition University (DAU) in its early period; programs that recognize a variety of development activities, such as the Defense Leadership and Management Program; single-purpose academic institutions, such as the Foreign Language Center of the Defense Language Institute; narrowly defined vocational courses of study, such as contract property disposition; and so forth. Some providers are operated by DoD, while others are state or nonprofit-sector institutions outside DoD. Some programs are cooperative efforts of DoD and non-DoD institutions, such as the graduate certificate programs offered jointly by the DAU and Florida Institute of Technology. Some ET&D offerings are provided by stand-alone organizations reporting to senior DoD leadership, while others exist merely as programs or courses embedded within DoD agencies.

A state system of higher education typically consists of a few major types of institutions, such as universities, community colleges, and vocational schools, although a wide diversity of programs is offered within these institutions. In this respect, the governance task facing DoD more closely resembles that of a state licensing agency, with its oversight responsibility for all of the diverse and unrelated nonprofit and for-profit providers operating in a state, combined with a corporate human resources (HR) department, with its ability to operate programs internally as well as to send employees to outside institutions.

Independent Evolution

The Departments of the Army and Navy have independent histories that are more than a century and a half longer than the relatively brief history of DoD and the Department of the Air Force. Within OSD, some agencies, such as the Defense Intelligence Agency, have relatively long histories, while others, such as the Missile Defense Agency, were recently created. Some ET&D providers, such as the Naval Postgraduate School, were originally founded to meet the needs of a single agency or department, while others, such as the Defense Acquisition University, were formed to centralize existing efforts across organizations. Thus, the various organizational elements of the DoD system of ET&D have evolved independently, with different missions and cultures. Calling such an aggregation of distinct entities a system represents an attempt to bring about better coordination, but this attempt comes from the top down, not from the institutions themselves.

In this respect, the governance challenge for DoD is similar to that of a corporation resulting from the merger of existing firms with very different organizational structures, corporate cultures, and standing networks of vendor relationships. However, the elements of DoD tend to be more thoroughly institutionalized, serve more diverse missions, and have more deeply committed stakeholders outside of the hierarchical chain of command than the elements of a for-profit conglomerate.

Hybrid Form

Although DoD itself could be viewed as a hierarchical organization because its authority derives from a single constitutional head and flows from the top down through a widening system of reporting branches, it departs considerably from a pure hierarchy. The military is often considered, by those unfamiliar with it, to be a model of hierarchical organization. In truth, the separation of operational command and administrative command is commonplace. The military pioneered matrix organization before the idea caught on in the business world. Even as a civilian organization, DoD consists of many quasi-independent organizations, each deriving its purpose from the overall DoD mission, but answering to a complex governance structure with command, funding, policy, and other accountability lines often going in different directions. To some extent, this is a general characteristic of American bureaucracy, resulting from generations of efforts to limit the potential for abuses of power (Wilson, 1989; Moe, 1995; and Light, 1997). In this respect, what is true of other executive departments seems especially true of the DoD, perhaps because of its enormous size, its history of interservice rivalries, and caution regarding the special trust placed in it as wielder of national power.

Within this loosely hierarchical multi-organizational system, the DoD system of ET&D is an even more complex case. It is a functional subsystem that cuts across organizational lines and primary missions. The governance relationships between providers and their key stakeholders include not only hierarchical lines of reporting but also market-oriented contracts involving competition; memoranda of agreement between members of consortia; the use of intermediaries, such as accrediting agencies and boards of visitors; and even informal cooperation between units that have no official relationship except up and down their "stove-piped" chains of command.

THE CHANCELLOR'S OFFICE

Amid a government-wide emphasis on improving performance, the Office of the Chancellor for Education and Professional Development in the DoD was established in 1998. The charter of this office establishes it as the principal advocate for the academic quality and cost-effectiveness of postsecondary ET&D provided to the DoD civilian workforce. In the DoD institutional context described above, the Chancellor's office is primarily concerned with the perspective of the functional sponsors, because they are the key stakeholders with the most direct interest in the value that ET&D can add to the workforce.

The Chancellor's office has little direct authority, yet it must promote its goals of quality and cost-effectiveness within this loosely coordinated system of diverse providers, employers, and stakeholders.

Levy et al. (2001a) discusses the strategic challenges facing the Chancellor's office in more detail and assesses the similarity of its situation to various other models, including other federal agencies, state boards of higher education, and corporate HR departments or corporate universities.

The present report focuses not on the governance role of the Chancellor's office alone but on the entire context of external governance within which the Chancellor's office seeks to advocate the quality and productivity of ET&D. The functional sponsors have more authority in DoD than does the Chancellor's office, yet in a system with multiple lines of governance, they also face limits to their influence over the provision of the ET&D required to achieve workforce objectives. The Chancellor's office seeks effective strategies for influencing the system, not only in its own advocacy role but also for possible adoption by functional sponsors and others. It sees an opportunity to contribute to the improvement of ET&D by helping sponsors overcome obstacles to their own governance of the institutions that serve them.

Chapter Three

THE STRUCTURAL ANALYSIS OF EXTERNAL GOVERNANCE

The first task in the strategic governance review is to gain a clear picture of the entities involved in governance and the relationships among them. The importance of this task rises in proportion to its difficulty. It will be relatively easy in a system with an organizational scheme that is either simple or already tightly coordinated, in which case the governance review may not be necessary. However, in a complex multi-organizational system with loose coordination, it may take considerable effort to disentangle the various strands of the governance network. This effort is justified if it enables system-level authorities and stakeholders to improve the responsiveness of the system to their governance, and thereby to improve their ability to achieve their goals. We suggest the following taxonomy as a way to begin talking about the structure of governance in the context of DoD ET&D.[1]

A TAXONOMY

In this section, we discuss the elements of external governance and provide a set of terms useful for making distinctions among these el-

---

[1]In this section, we attempt to achieve consistency with current thinking in organizational theory, higher education, and other literature on governance. However, the primary criteria for this framework are its applicability to the DoD context and its usefulness in helping DoD leaders to understand the governance of ET&D in a new light. Thus, while we hope this material proves useful as a starting point for understanding other systems of ET&D, it is intended neither as a generic model of multi-organizational systems nor as a rigorous foundation for theoretical work.

ements. After defining external governance itself, we describe the entities involved in governance, functions of governance, and domains of ET&D subject to governance.

External Governance

For the purpose of this strategic review, we define *external governance* as a set of relationships between providers of ET&D and the stakeholders that exert influence over the nature, quality, and cost-effectiveness of the education offered.

This definition excludes *internal governance*, the role of decisionmakers within the provider organization. The terms used to identify internal versus external governance vary among types of organizations. In corporations, the function of making decisions for the organization is called *management*, while the function of overseeing management is called *governance*. In government organizations, the internal role is often called *administration*, while the external roles have been called various things, including *government, governance*, and *oversight*. In higher education, decisionmaking is often shared between the administration and the faculty, with substantial inputs from other stakeholders, and the term *governance* is often used to describe both internal and external roles.

External governance of ET&D clearly includes outside organizations such as boards of visitors and accrediting bodies. The case of students and student unions raises some ambiguity; we treat these as external unless they have achieved formal decisionmaking status within the provider organization. In a complex system, where the provider resides under a larger organizational umbrella such as DoD or a conglomerate corporation, the senior management and the other components of the larger organization are considered to be external to the provider.

Formal governance arrangements are structural relationships between providers and stakeholders where the identity, governance role, and domain of influence of the stakeholders are officially established and documented. For example, the relationship between a provider within DoD and its command sponsor is a formal arrangement.

Informal governance arrangements are relationships between providers and stakeholders where the specific nature of the influence is not officially established and documented, but the relationship is acknowledged and implicitly accepted as legitimate.[2] An informal arrangement may supersede a formal arrangement when the original authorizing document becomes outdated. The new arrangement may become formalized at a later date upon the issuance of a revised document. The relationship between a provider and a functional sponsor is sometimes informal rather than formal, because the exact nature of the relationship is not always made explicit in directives.

Actual influence relationships are operational relationships between providers and the stakeholders that influence them, regardless of whether there is a recognized arrangement or not.

It is possible to have a governance arrangement with little actual influence, and it is possible to have considerable influence without a formal or informal arrangement. Formal and informal arrangements are emphasized in the structural analysis presented in this chapter, while actual relationships are emphasized in the implementation audit presented in Chapter Four.

Providers

Providers are organizations or suborganizations that provide ET&D directly to students. These include institutions of higher education, but they also may include specific programs within institutions, programs that bridge multiple institutions, courses of instruction, and educational activities within organizations that are not primarily educational.[3] Under this definition, the Naval Postgraduate School, the

---

[2]We have defined *governance* in terms of influence rather than formal or legitimate authority. Legitimacy and influence are both dimensions along which stakeholders vary (Mitchell et al., 1997). However, influence may be observed in practice, but defining legitimacy requires an act of judgment that depends on the system context and the perspective of the entity sponsoring the analysis. Rather than asserting such a broad judgment, we rely on the scope of this project relative to the mission of the Chancellor's office and focus on those interorganizational relationships that may influence the academic quality and cost-effectiveness of ET&D. This allows us to make the operational and functional distinctions in this chapter.

[3]In higher education, the term *institutions* is generally used for what we call *providers*. However, our taxonomy is intended primarily as a way of describing the DoD context,

Defense Leadership and Management Program, and Defense Finance and Accounting Service Career Learning Centers are all examples of providers. Providers can be thought of as the supply side of ET&D.

Stakeholders

Stakeholders are any persons or organizations that are external to the providers of ET&D but have concerns or interests in, obtain benefits from, or conduct governance roles with respect to providers and the ET&D they provide.[4] Examples of stakeholders include students and their employers; command and other sponsors; and intermediary organizations, such as accrediting commissions.

Systems

As illustrated in Figure 3.1, *systems* are sets of related providers and the stakeholders concerned with or exerting governance over them and the ET&D they provide. In this analysis, we restrict the meaning of *system* to entities that share a common mission or purpose in which ET&D is important, even if the entities also have separate individual missions or purposes other than ET&D.[5] Systems of ET&D

---

where providers may consist of programs and courses that exist apart from any institution of higher education.

[4]Stakeholder theory is found originally in the private-sector theory and literature on strategic management of the firm (Ackoff, 1981; and Freeman, 1984). They use the term *stakeholder* to identify all those who have interests in or influence over the firm's activities, not limited to shareholders or owners. Scholl (2002) finds that stakeholder concepts are useful for analyzing management in public-sector settings.

Stakeholder analysis is a technique for identifying stakeholders and assessing their importance (Mitchell et al., 1997; Management Sciences for Health and United Nations Children's Fund, 1998; and Overseas Development Administration, 1995). It differs from the structural analysis of governance described in this report primarily because it takes the point of view of the influenced entity seeking to understand its environment, rather than that of a system-level authority seeking to understand and improve the system. Nevertheless, there are many overlaps. Stakeholder literature provides more detailed models than the approach described in this report.

[5]This use of *systems* bears strong resemblance to the use of *networks* to describe multi-organizational phenomena (Jones, Hesterly, and Borgatti, 1997; and Alter and Hage, 1993). However, we focus here on systems with an external purpose, something that is not necessarily part of the network concept. We also find that the DoD system of ET&D is neither a pure network nor a pure hierarchy, as those terms are often con-

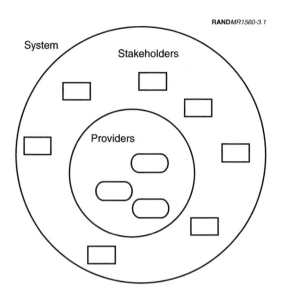

RAND*MR1560-3.1*

Figure 3.1—A Multi-Organizational System of ET&D

are open systems.[6] Thus, they may overlap; the U.S. government is a system, DoD is a system within the government, and the acquisition community is a system within DoD. The network of ET&D providers and stakeholders within DoD is also a system, as is, on a smaller scale, the Defense Acquisition University.

Special Stakeholder Types

One way to seek greater understanding of governance of an array of providers and stakeholders in a complex system might be to catego-

---

trasted, but rather a hybrid of network, hierarchy, and market-like organizational elements.

[6]Systems may be characterized as closed or open. A closed system is one in which all influences and effects are contained within the system; it is more of a theoretical model than a real world phenomenon. On the other hand, an open system is one that may be influenced by, and have effects on, entities that are outside of its formal boundaries (Chavis, Florin, and Felix, 1993). Put another way, if a system is a set of entities that influence each other, an open system is one without fixed boundaries; new entities enter as they gain influence over or are affected by the rest of the system.

rize these entities in increasing detail. Unfortunately, any strict categorical scheme is likely to run aground on the reality that the members of such a system often perform multiple overlapping roles and functions. The approach taken here is to focus on the roles and functions rather than to categorize the stakeholders themselves. However, there are certain types of stakeholders worth special emphasis. These should not be thought of as categories, but as important players that might be overlooked in applying general methods of governance and stakeholder analysis to the specific context of ET&D within DoD.

Demand-Side Stakeholders. These are the individuals and organizations that receive the primary benefits of ET&D from providers, particularly, actual or potential students and their actual or potential employers.

In market-driven systems (not just ET&D), customers are the demand-side stakeholders, but in theory they do not require special governance arrangements because the competitive power of the market enforces their interests. However, wherever markets are less than perfect, customers may benefit from individual or collective governance relationships with providers.[7]

In traditional higher education, students are the customers. They typically choose their own providers, attend school as independent agents, and negotiate their own employment upon graduation. Current students are often formally recognized through elected representatives as a component of internal governance, and former students (alumni) are sometimes active in external governance. Furthermore, the ET&D interests of potential employers may influence providers only indirectly, mediated by the decisions of students who expect to get jobs in the future and communicated to providers through advisory boards and industry representatives.

On the other hand, in workforce-oriented ET&D contexts such as corporations or DoD, students are generally employees and are

---

[7]Markets may be imperfect, for example, when information is asymmetric between parties, when purchasing decisions are made by parties other than those receiving the primary benefits, and inside partially hierarchical organizations. The field of transaction cost economics shows that such demand-side governance relationships are common in real-world markets and organizations (Williamson, 1996).

sponsored or authorized by their employers.[8] This means that their present or potential employers are important customers of ET&D as entities that receive workforce benefits from the ET&D of workers. Thus, our analysis emphasizes the employer rather than the student as the key demand-side stakeholder, although without excluding consideration of student concerns and satisfaction.

For practical analysis this type of stakeholder consists not of DoD as a whole, but of the operational unit within DoD where the decision to authorize the student's training is made and/or where the workforce need for such training exists. It is the unit that loses the services of the student during full-time training activities and/or the unit that gains the benefit of the student's increased skill and understanding after the training. When a Defense Contract Audit Agency (DCAA) auditor receives training from the Defense Contract Audit Institute, the employer is not just DCAA but the Field Audit Office (FAO) or regional office where the employee works. If training makes it possible for a valued employee to move from the FAO to the regional office, the FAO loses an employee even though DCAA as a whole gains from the training.

Clearly, a conflict of interest may arise when the unit sponsoring the student or funding the training is different from the units that may potentially obtain the student's services following training. As an example, the Chief Financial Officers Fellows Program serves financial officers from across DoD, and program participants may go wherever they choose when they finish the training. While training costs are paid by the agency that sponsors the training, the employee's salary continues to be paid by the parent agency during training. Such situations emphasize the need for a system-level approach to ET&D in a multi-organizational system.

In DoD, the interests of functionally related employers are represented by functional sponsors. Thus, functional sponsors should be

---

[8]In this report, focusing on the DoD workforce, the terms *students* and *employees* usually refer to the same people. However, providers that participate in the DoD system may in some cases enroll foreign civilian or military personnel, dependents of DoD personnel, and American civilians unconnected with DoD. For a functional analysis, it is useful to maintain the distinction between the role of students with respect to providers of ET&D and the role of employees with respect to DoD.

considered as key demand-side stakeholders in any governance re-view for the DoD system of ET&D.

System-Level Stakeholders. These are the individuals or organiza-tions designated with some degree of responsibility for the mission of an entire system.

The definition of an open system entails ambiguity between a system that pursues its mission as derived from an external authority and the larger system with the authority to assign that mission. For ex-ample, all DoD activities serve the national security mission obtained from the Constitution and the President as Commander in Chief, but it is not necessary to mention this every time a particular system within DoD is described. A system-level stakeholder is anyone through whom this externally assigned mission is delegated, such as a command sponsor in DoD or a general manager in the corporate context. Such stakeholders should be highlighted to ensure inter-preting the system according to its overall mission rather than just balancing stakeholder interests that may or may not be mission ori-ented.[9] Note that this type of stakeholder is defined in terms of the nature of its interest and not the degree of its influence; system-level

---

[9]Most of the governance and stakeholder literature paints a picture of multiple com-peting external interests, and a single focal point of decisionmaking for the firm or or-ganization (Oudman et al., 1998). It assumes either the point of view of an external stakeholder looking inward and seeking influence or the point of view of the organiza-tion itself looking at all of the competing interests in its environment. Thus, the only global perspective is that of the organization looking outward—through the eyes of management/internal governance or of a single dominant stakeholder (Savage et al., 1997; and Tirole, 2001). This literature is readily applicable to the analysis of a single provider of ET&D and its stakeholders.

However, the picture painted by such literature is less applicable to a multi-organiza-tional system of ET&D serving a higher externally derived mission, as we have de-scribed in the DoD context. What is missing is the system-level perspective that this strategic governance review seeks to serve, a global perspective that looks inward at the providers and their relationships with various key stakeholders.

Some of the literature on democratic governance of public institutions takes such a global perspective looking in. Behn (2001) suggests the concept of 360-degree ac-countability for public organizations in a network of mutual responsibility as an alter-native to the hierarchical model of accountability. Without getting into the theoretical issues Behn raises, the present report is an attempt to help DoD begin investigating how shared governance actually works and might be improved within an ET&D sys-tem that is neither a pure hierarchy nor a fulfillment of Behn's network concept of mu-tual accountability relationships.

responsibility is not necessarily linked with dominant power over the system.

In a system with ET&D as its primary mission, the system-level stakeholders are likely also to be demand-side stakeholders, or at least to be designated as representatives of a class of demand-side stakeholders. However, in a complex system where ET&D provision cuts across the hierarchical boundaries of organizations with primary missions other than ET&D, the needs of demand-side stakeholders may not be salient in the priorities of system-level stakeholders. Thus, it is useful to distinguish between the roles, even though they may often be assigned to the same office.

Peripheral Stakeholders. These are individuals or organizations that have goals, interests, or concerns at stake in the provision of ET&D other than the central mission of the system and other than obtaining the direct benefits of ET&D as employers of students.

Various entities may have peripheral stakes in workforce ET&D. An example is the Office of Management and Budget (OMB), which establishes rules and regulations for carrying out Circular A-76. Individual agencies employ and/or train the staff who execute A-76 studies, while OMB has a clear stake in the content of A-76–related ET&D without actually employing such trained staff—and without power to enforce how the training is carried out. Another example is the developers of computer systems for various DoD activities; they have clear stakes in the proper training of employees who will use such systems, but they do not take on mission-level responsibility for those employees and their employers.

Note that a single entity might represent workforce demand with respect to one provider or domain and peripheral interests with respect to other providers or domains.

Intermediaries. These are individuals or organizations that exercise influence over a provider, system, or stakeholders on behalf of other stakeholders, rather than primarily in pursuit of their own goals, concerns, or interests.

Examples of stakeholders in this category include accrediting bodies, advisory boards, and the Chancellor's office. We have already discussed the importance of demand-side and system-level stakeholders; such parties often depend on intermediaries to represent their interests in dealing with providers. Gates et al. (2001) emphasizes the role of intermediaries in ensuring the quality and productivity of ET&D.

An organization may simultaneously fit into multiple stakeholder descriptions depending on its relationship to providers and the roles it plays. For instance, a university is clearly a provider of higher education, but it is also an employer of teachers with advanced degrees and, thus, a stakeholder with respect to other universities. Within DoD, a single office like the Office of the Under Secretary of Defense for Acquisition, Technology, and Logistics [USD(AT&L)] can simultaneously be a resource and functional sponsor with regard to one field of ET&D, such as acquisition, while also being an employer with regard to another field, such as financial management. Thus, these labels are a matter of what "hat" an entity is wearing, rather than intrinsic characteristics.

Stakeholder Influence

Stakeholders vary in the degree and nature of their influence over the providers of ET&D. Mitchell et al. (1997) identifies three dimensions on which stakeholder salience could be measured when performing stakeholder analysis from the perspective of the organization looking outward: legitimacy, urgency, and power. The strategic governance review described in this report takes a system-level perspective rather than a component-level perspective, so the importance of stakeholders in the review should be based on the priorities of the system-level stakeholder authorizing the review.

Interorganizational influence is another aspect of stakeholder relationships that we have examined in more depth and reported on in Augustine et al. (2002). Three findings of that work are relevant here:

1. The power or influence of a stakeholder over providers of ET&D in a multi-organizational system forms a continuum between strong and weak influence over various domains, and a stakeholder's influence may shift not only as its own characteristics change but also as the provider and the context change. Thus, the degree of influence is not a defining category but a useful dimension on

which to evaluate stakeholder effectiveness, as in the audit described in Chapter Four.

2. Stakeholder influence is not simply a matter of disciplinary authority or resource provision, as often emphasized in governance discussions, but it also includes other, more socially mediated forms of influence such as expert, referent, and legitimate power. A stakeholder should not be neglected in this analysis simply because it lacks the power to reward or punish. On the other hand, a stakeholder with dominant power over providers, such as a command sponsor with the authority to issue and enforce directives, must be accounted for in any analysis of less influential stakeholders.

3. A stakeholder may have indirect influence over a provider through its influence over intermediaries and other stakeholders. The structural analysis should identify not only individual stakeholders and their relationships with providers, but also their relationships with each other in a network of formal and informal governance arrangements.

Governance Functions

Because external governance consists of various forms of influence in addition to command authority and can reside in informal as well as formal arrangements, we find it useful to frame the structural analysis in terms of governance functions. These are the tasks that stakeholders carry out within the system, and they reflect the values that the organizations engaged in governance hold vis-a-vis the ET&D system. There are various ways to categorize governance functions; for the structural analysis, a simple classification scheme seems most useful. The following categories are quite broad, often overlap in operation, and do not necessarily constitute an exhaustive list.

Command and Control. This is the function of enforcing rules and decisions, overseeing implementation, and/or scrutinizing deviations. It is governance in the strongest sense, embodied in the chain of command. It is associated with, but not equivalent to, a dominant degree of power or influence. In practice, such a linkage between the function and the power to carry it out cannot be assumed in advance and should be verified on a case-by-case basis.

There are two equally important aspects to command and control—giving authoritative directions (command), and overseeing and monitoring to ensure directions are followed, deviations are corrected, and actual results are accounted for in subsequent decisions (control). The control function of governance may carry considerable influence even without specific power to punish deviations, since many desirable outcomes depend on favorable rather than unfavorable reports. While a compliance auditor such as a Certified Public Accountant firm or an Inspector General's office does not issue commands, it is an intermediary that serves a control function in this sense.

Resource Provision. This function refers to influencing another organization by providing resources on which it depends but without direct decisionmaking authority over that organization (Pfeffer and Salancik, 1978). This can be seen in the resource sponsor's control of the flow of funds or the functional sponsor's control of the flow of students to an ET&D provider in cases where these sponsors are not simultaneously the command sponsors. Although an accrediting agency's primary governance function is evaluation, it also controls a resource that is critical for many providers, namely, legitimacy in the higher education sector.

Coordination and/or Communication. This is the function of facilitating cooperation between elements of a system. Coordination implies taking an active operational role such as scheduling events and assigning tasks; communication implies a less assertive role, such as acting as a liaison between organizations. These roles may be performed by stakeholders that have command authority or control of resources, but are not limited to such stakeholders.[10] Coordinating boards in higher education, such as the California Postsecondary Education Commission, enable schools to align their

---

[10]Coordination and communication functions may also be performed spontaneously by the members of a network of organizations in pursuit of their own goals, rather than necessarily by a stakeholder engaged in external governance (Chisholm, 1989).

programs with each other and with the interests of various other stakeholders. Accrediting agencies and the Chancellor's office sponsor conferences and disseminate information about quality in ET&D.

Evaluation, Research, Planning, Advising, and/or Advocacy. There remains a cluster of mission-support roles not included as such in the first three categories, although in many cases these tasks also assist communication, provide important resources, or support the command-and-control function. These are functions that a stakeholder might perform either in pursuit of its own goals (e.g., a functional sponsor's involvement in planning future student loads) or as an intermediary (e.g., an accrediting agency's evaluation of educational programs).

Domains

A *domain* is a coherent area of interest and operational decisionmaking within a system of ET&D. Domains are the elements of ET&D provision that stakeholders seek to influence. Examples of domains include mission, structure, operations, services, curriculum content, instructional methods and materials, personnel, and admissions. These domains can be influenced at various levels, including system, institution, school, department, unit, program, and course.

At times, external governance will focus on a single domain or cluster of domains, but at the system level it may focus on many domains. For instance, a resource sponsor will be explicitly interested in finance as a domain. A functional sponsor may be more interested in faculty, curriculum, and admissions than in research or finance. But an analysis from the perspective of the DoD system of ET&D as a whole could include all domains.

Figure 3.2 illustrates a simplified case of governance involving a provider and four stakeholders. It also shows how these entities relate to each other through governance functions that apply to specific domains of ET&D.

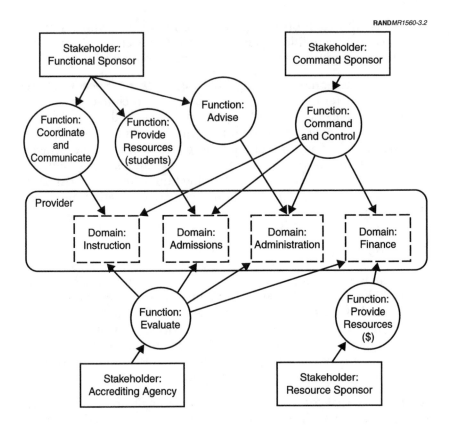

RAND*MR1560-3.2*

Figure 3.2—Examples of Stakeholders, Governance Functions, and
Domains of ET&D

MAPPING GOVERNANCE ARRANGEMENTS

Given the above taxonomy, mapping external governance structures
is straightforward. It starts with four questions:

1. Who are the providers in the ET&D system under review?

2. Who are the stakeholders (including intermediaries) involved in
   or interested in external governance for these providers?

3. What governance functions are performed by each of these stake-holders?

4. Over what domains do these stakeholders exercise or seek influence?

In a well-structured, formally arranged system, such a map will already exist and be familiar to leaders; in a loosely coordinated, multi-organizational system, as described above, or a self-organizing system, the effort of creating such a map may provide new and valuable insights into the implicit organizational design of the system.

Sources of Information

Unlike an audit, this structural analysis does not require gathering data in the field. The information for mapping governance arrangements will be obtained from two primary sources:

First, *documents* provide information about formal governance arrangements. For DoD providers, the authorizing directives and instructions identify the command and resource sponsors and often also describe the functional sponsor and various advisory relationships. Of course, providers should be able to show documents identifying their formal relationships, but it may be desirable to perform this strategic analysis without involving providers. Many institutions now provide links to such documents on their websites.

Second, the *personal knowledge* of administrators provides information about informal governance arrangements. Administrators with extensive experience in a system usually possess a great amount of knowledge about how the system works. However, such people may not realize what they know, or they may not realize that their assumptions about governance arrangements do not match the documented formal structures. Thus, it may be helpful to elicit such tacit knowledge by first sketching out the formal arrangements as found in documents and then asking administrators for feedback as to the accuracy and currency of these structures.

Cataloging Arrangements

The analysis proceeds by asking a series of questions about governance arrangements. The answers to these questions will constitute a catalog of entities, functions, and domains that will form the basis for further stages in the governance review.

Who are the providers in the ET&D system under review? The providers included in the scope of the analysis should be identified at an early stage. In the case of ET&D, the scope might consist of a single provider or a defined set of similar providers, such as providers of leadership training programs. But it might also include an overall system of related providers, such as the entire program of developing analytical and leadership skills for potential high-level leaders in the DoD. When the analysis is conducted from a system-level perspective in a context with overlapping systems and subsystems, it is important to establish the level at which the system is defined. Defining the scope in terms of specific providers will guide the distinction between internal and external governance.[11]

Who are the stakeholders involved in or interested in external governance for these providers? This question may be answered according to the specific types of stakeholders described above:

- What employers' workforce needs are supposed to be served by the providers in the scope of the ET&D system under review?

- What system-level stakeholders exercise governance over the overall mission of the system comprised of these providers?

- What peripheral stakeholders also have interests in aspects of the ET&D provided?

- What intermediaries perform governance roles with respect to these providers and the other stakeholders identified?

---

[11]In some cases, reviewers may not at first be aware of all the providers serving the needs of the stakeholders emphasized in the review. For simplicity, we start with providers and proceed to stakeholders, but that is not the only approach. An alternative approach might start by identifying specific stakeholders and then catalog the providers that serve them. In either case, a reiterative procedure may be followed, identifying stakeholders and providers in turn until a satisfactory listing is created.

As noted previously, a given entity could be listed in the answers to more than one question above. The USD(AT&L) serves as a system-level authority for the DAU, as the employer (in a broad sense) of many but certainly not all acquisition personnel, and as an interme-diary representing other DoD employers of acquisition personnel through functional sponsorship of acquisition ET&D.

What governance functions are performed by each of these stake-holders? This item seeks to flesh out the picture of governance with a rough impression of the role of each player, using a simple but useful scheme.

The four general categories described above should give enough de-tail for this purpose:

- command and control

- resource provision

- coordination and/or communication

- other support functions (evaluation, research, planning, advis-ing, and/or advocacy).

Over what domains do these stakeholders exercise or seek influ-ence? This step is optional; in some cases, listing the stakeholders and their governance functions is enough to answer the important questions and clarify the governance picture for system planners. In other cases, only certain domains are of interest in the review, and the stakeholders that are not involved in those domains may be ex-cluded from further analysis. For instance, a review concerned with academic quality will not need to dwell on resource sponsors unless it becomes clear that their influence is or could be critical to aca-demic quality. Later, in the step of aligning governance, this linkage of stakeholders, functions, and domains will be used as the starting point for asking whether key stakeholder goals are appropriately covered by the existing governance arrangements.

Drawing a Governance Map

For greater insight, the general relationships may be represented graphically on a map of the external governance network under review. This should be done at an appropriate scale and level of detail; time should not be wasted mapping in perfect detail all of the information in the catalog of stakeholders, functions, and domains. One way to simplify the map is to group together stakeholders that are similar or act in concert for shared goals. Different categories of influence can be shown graphically. In a complex system with many providers, it may be necessary to portray only a portion of the system on any one diagram. See Figure 3.3 for an example of a governance map showing a single provider and the stakeholders in direct relationship with it.

The map's purpose is to provide planners with a broad perspective and a sense of the relative complexity or simplicity of the governance network under review. Such a mapping might identify existing and potential alliances between entities that share interests. On the other hand, it might show that competition exists between entities, especially with regard to the reporting burden on the provider.

Mapping Indirect Governance Relationships

The above questions focus on stakeholders in direct relationship to the providers under review. However, there are also indirect relationships that contribute to external governance in the system. These include the relationships of intermediaries with the stakeholders they represent as well as any governance-related interactions among stakeholders. Identifying indirect relationships creates an opportunity to identify stakeholders that are involved in governance but do not interact directly with providers. Adding such stakeholders and relationships to the governance map shows clearly how governance in a multi-organizational system becomes increasingly complex with the addition of more channels of governance. Figure 3.4 shows the same one-provider system shown in Figure 3.3, but with indirect governance relationships and indirectly linked stakeholders added to the map. It also represents the system symbolically as a line around the map, dashed rather than solid because systems of ET&D are open systems that interact in myriad ways with the society and the organizational context around them.

Mapping indirect governance relationships requires asking two additional questions.

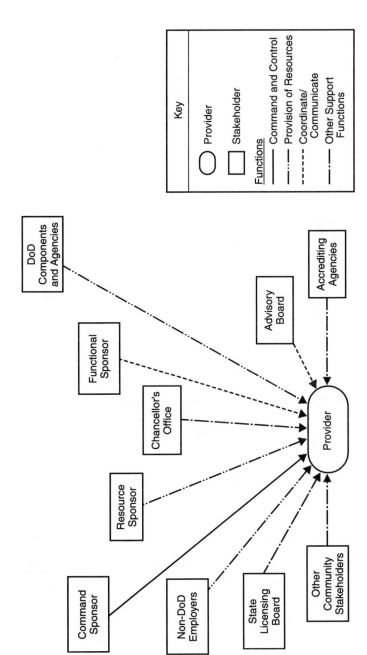

Figure 3.3—External Governance Map for a Single Provider—Direct Links

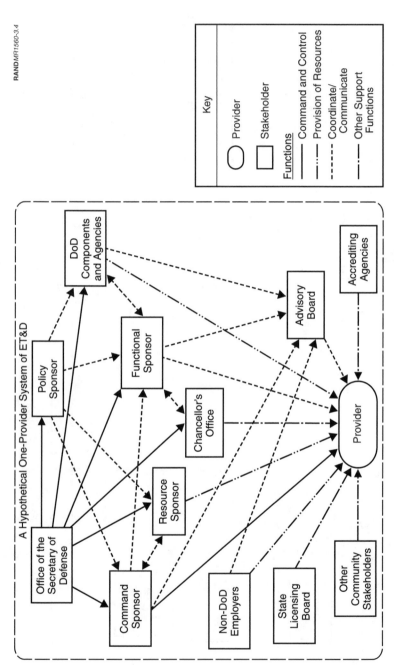

Figure 3.4—External Governance Map for a Single Provider—with Indirect Links and System Included

What other stakeholders do intermediaries represent? Peripheral stakeholders and employers who receive trained employees but do not sponsor students may not perform any governance function that links them directly with providers, yet they expect their needs and interests to be served by the system. Such parties usually have intermediaries to represent their interests through governance functions. In addition, some stakeholders that perform one governance function might find it efficient to employ an intermediary to perform other governance functions in which it is interested. The OSD is a system-level stakeholder with a command-and-control role over many ET&D activities, but does not wish to specialize in the evaluation of ET&D quality. Thus, it has instructed DoD institutions to pursue accreditation, using accrediting agencies as intermediaries to ensure that providers deliver an acceptable quality of education and training.

The mapping task requires linking all relevant stakeholders with the intermediaries that represent them, and vice versa. At times, this will reveal that the initial list was incomplete, and another stakeholder or intermediary will be identified by this linkage. To follow our example, a complete map would show the OSD as a system-level stakeholder represented by accrediting agencies as intermediaries.

Some organizations that might at first appear to be intermediaries actually perform internal governance functions in service of the provider rather than represent an external stakeholder. For example, a research firm may be hired by the administration to assist in planning. It may be considered as an extension of the provider and excluded from this analysis, unless its role points to a salient weakness or gap in external governance. If the latter, it should be noted for follow-up in the task of aligning governance arrangements with stakeholder goals, which is described later in this chapter.

Depending on the purpose of the review, extra effort might be put into this step by drilling down into the membership of intermediary boards and committees to discover what stakeholders are represented there. This is standard practice in the analysis of corporate governance, where board membership generally carries more power than membership on advisory and governing boards in higher education. However, this information might benefit an analysis of ET&D

governance by revealing previously unrecognized sources of conflict or opportunities for alliances.

What interactions among stakeholders (including intermediaries) are relevant to the governance of ET&D? Having identified the providers and stakeholders, including intermediaries and the stakeholders behind them, it should be possible to trace a line of governance—i.e., influence—from each stakeholder on the map to a provider of ET&D. Such a drawing gives the wrong impression, though, because in a multi-organizational system of any significant complexity, there are likely to be multiple interactions among organizations, and multiple channels of influence among stakeholders and providers. Identifying such linkages better reveals the pattern of strong and weak influences over ET&D outcomes. It is a necessary step if planners intend to align governance functions with stakeholder goals, as described in the latter part of this chapter.

Some caution is warranted in mapping such interactions. Not every relationship is relevant to the governance of the domains of ET&D emphasized in this structural analysis. The Departments of the Army, Navy, and Air Force clearly interact for a number of reasons; what is relevant to this analysis is whether and how they interact for the governance of ET&D. The Defense Language Institute Foreign Language Center (DLIFLC) is subject to governance by both the Army's Training and Doctrine Command and the Assistant Secretary of Defense for Command, Control, Communications, and Intelligence. These two stakeholders must communicate and coordinate with each other, and thus each has two lines of influence on the DLIFLC: one directly to the provider and one indirectly through the other party. Generating a greater awareness of such multiple channels of governance may provide one of the most useful benefits of the structural analysis, showing opportunities for shared influence over the quality and productivity of ET&D.

Additional Lessons from the Mapping Exercise

At this point, after the mapping of governance arrangements but prior to the attempt to align them with stakeholder goals, the primary benefit of the exercise to system-level planners lies in any insights they have gained into the nature and pattern of governance relationships. At least two additional questions can be addressed based on this global overview of the governance structure.

Is the governance structure formally documented? When there are strong informal governance arrangements other than the documented formal arrangements, one of two conditions is likely to hold. The documents that specify formal arrangements may have become outdated as informal arrangements adapted to changing organizational goals and environment. In such cases, documenting the informal arrangements can help systematize and preserve the personal knowledge of administrators familiar with the new arrangements. Another possibility is that the informal arrangements may have strayed from the intent of the originally specified formal arrangements. In such cases, systematically reviewing the original documents provides a foundation for bringing the governance structure back into compliance. In either case, the research that underlies the mapping process will reveal whether there is a problem with inconsistency between formal and informal arrangements.

Is the governance structure simple and clear? A well-drawn governance map provides compelling visual evidence as to the simplicity or complexity of the network of relationships it represents. This evidence is only meaningful in comparisons between systems drawn to similar levels of detail; an intuitive judgment of complexity or simplicity might be an artifact of the scale of the map or the level of detail. However, a comparative approach can be useful in reviewing different subsystems within a larger system; highlighting changes over time within one system; or evaluating prospective changes, such as the addition of a new intermediary to an existing system.

ALIGNING GOVERNANCE ARRANGEMENTS

Once governance arrangements have been mapped, system planners may wish to proceed with the task of aligning those arrangements with stakeholder goals—evaluating whether there are gaps, overlaps, or other misalignments in the governance coverage of key goals. This step starts with the identification of key stakeholders and their goals and then matches the goals with the governance functions that support them. The analysis proceeds through the following series of questions.

Which of the stakeholders previously identified are the key stakeholders for this task? Given the map or catalog generated above, this step determines which stakeholders really matter for the purpose of the task of alignment. The list should be relatively short to keep the analysis manageable. The number of people or organizations that have an interest in a system of ET&D is potentially very large, and choosing which ones to exclude requires an exercise of judgment.

This selection should be guided by the stakeholder that authorized the review and based on the purpose of the review. It might be based on a selection of domains; as discussed previously, a review of governance regarding quality of education would have little concern for resource sponsors as financial stakeholders. Excluding them from this list does not imply that they do not matter, merely that they are not a high priority for the analysis.

In the DoD system of ET&D, a review conducted by the Chancellor's office would be guided by its mission to advocate academic quality and productivity and by its focus on functional sponsors as the primary beneficiaries of ET&D. Thus, the functional sponsors would be identified as key stakeholders the goals of which are to be analyzed, while other types of stakeholders might be de-emphasized in the analysis.

What are the key goals of these key stakeholders? For each key stakeholder identified in the previous step, this step lists the central goals that are at stake in this system of ET&D. These goals might be found in official documents, deduced from the nature and mission of the organization, and/or learned from conversations with leaders and administrators.

The list should be targeted at a level of abstraction appropriate for talking about governance functions, focusing on broad and enduring goals rather than operational and changing objectives. As a guide, we suggest broad categories of goals for a system of ET&D. These are not definitive, but are intended to stimulate further thinking about goals. The categories are as follows:

- *Providing/obtaining a skilled workforce (effectiveness or quality).* Providing a skilled workforce is a goal arising from the mission of an ET&D system; obtaining a skilled workforce is a goal arising from the interests of employers as key stakeholders. A forward-thinking employer needs a reliable flow of skilled personnel and thus has a major stake in the system of ET&D that provides that flow. At times, this need may be so great and so difficult to fill from existing providers that an employer will create a new organization or program to obtain a reliable source of workers.

This goal may have several subgoals:

— *Providing/obtaining the needed number of skilled workers over time.* Employers and workforce planners have a stake in the quantity of workers receiving ET&D in each field and in scheduling the flow of workers to meet changing workforce plans and needs.

— *Providing/obtaining the appropriate content of ET&D.* Personnel must be trained in the needed skills, according to current standards. This is clearly in the interest of employers, but also of other stakeholders such as an agency that has responsibility for setting technical standards in a field. An organization dependent on standardized technology has a strong interest in the standardization of content in any ET&D regarding the use of that technology.

— *Providing/obtaining the desired quality of ET&D.* The overarching system may place a premium on quality as a value and as a reflection of the importance of its mission. Within the system, employers may also emphasize the quality of ET&D if they believe that it results in a higher-quality workforce. Intermediaries such as accrediting agencies or the Chancellor's office may have this goal as part of their mission and values.

The above three subgoals—quantity, quality, and appropriateness—could be considered aspects of effectiveness as a value and as a stakeholder interest.

• *Making efficient use of resources (cost-effectiveness or productivity).* The provision of ET&D requires resources, and the efficient use of those resources is a major goal. Efficiency in the sense of saving money is clearly in the interest of any stakeholders that provide funds. However, efficiency in the sense of achieving more and greater results with the resources available is a mission-based goal of the entire system of ET&D.

- *Maintaining a high quality of life for employees (students).* The system and some stakeholders may set standards for quality of life, based on values and/or on the belief that higher quality of life results in a higher-quality workforce. Thus, goals might include ensuring the adequate provision of services such as health care, child care, transportation, and housing while attending school; and ensuring students a reasonable balance of personal time and course requirements (and work load if students are not fully released from work obligations while attending school). A related concern might be to ensure that personnel are appropriately rewarded for their efforts.

- *Maintaining equity, or fairness.* Public agencies exist to serve the public interest, and like other public agencies, DoD has institutional values regarding equal opportunity and access for individuals, which must be met by any provider in the system.

Finally, many operational goals arise from other, higher goals, such as those we have suggested. An attempt should be made, when constructing the list of key goals for the structural analysis, to trace such instrumental goals back to the primary goals they serve.

Who is performing what governance functions relative to the key stakeholder goals? For each of the key goals selected above, this question identifies the existing governance arrangements in two dimensions: first, who is acting on behalf of the stakeholders to protect the goal, and second, what governance functions are being performed regarding this goal? Answers to these questions may be obtained quickly by reference to the system map created earlier. To illustrate using the example of the subgoal "providing/obtaining the desired quality of ET&D," an accrediting agency is an intermediary focused on this goal, and the governance function it performs in pursuit of that goal is evaluation. Functional sponsors within DoD work toward "providing/obtaining the appropriate content of ET&D" in part through their membership in curriculum oversight boards. Such boards perform an advisory function as intermediaries.

By the end of this stage, the analysis will have produced a list of the key goals of the system, the stakeholders who care about these goals, the identity of intermediaries and other stakeholders who are acting to protect the goals, and the governance functions being performed in pursuit of the goals.

What are the obstacles or threats to the achievements of these goals? We are now moving beyond the mapping and categorization of governance and beginning to generate information about specific goals that will be useful in efforts to improve the effectiveness of governance. When the relative need for governance functions to support specific goals is considered, it is highly relevant to ask why those goals might not be fulfilled without sufficient governance.

- Does the system possess the institutional capacity to achieve these goals? If not, could the capacity be developed, given more effective governance?

- Do the interests and goals of the provider organization and its leaders conflict with the goals or reinforce them? Conflict suggests a need for explicit governance arrangements or a better job of structuring incentives within the system, while reinforcement suggests a self-governing mechanism may be at work.

- Do the interests and goals of other stakeholders conflict with the goals or reinforce them? Where there is conflict, a governance role of mediation or policy setting at a higher level may be necessary to resolve differences. Where there is reinforcement, multiple stakeholders may be able to cooperate, perhaps through a coordinating intermediary, for more efficient and effective governance.

- Are the goals currently being met? Do they have a consistent history of being met?

Any goals that are congruent with the interests and goals of the provider and other stakeholders, that are currently being met, and that have been consistently met in the past are already either self governing or well governed and do not need further review (unless the purpose of the analysis is to study areas of good governance for insights and successful practices).

Are there significant gaps and/or overlaps in coverage of key goals and functions? Finally, this analysis examines opportunities for improving the governance of the system by filling gaps in the coverage of key goals with governance arrangements, reducing overlaps in the coverage, reconciling conflicts between goals, and identifying opportunities for cooperation between stakeholders.

Are any key goals *not* being addressed for a stakeholder or for the system as a whole? If so, what are the consequences of such a deficiency? What governance functions are needed to address these goals? What sort of governance arrangement would be appropriate in this context? This set of questions focuses on opportunities to improve the effectiveness of governance by plugging gaps in the coverage of key goals.

Are there specific goals that are shared among stakeholders? Are there obvious redundancies among the governance functions performed by stakeholders addressing the goals? Are there clear opportunities for strategic partnerships between stakeholders, for collective action through intermediaries, or for indirect influence through some party with a more direct governance function? This set of questions seeks to improve the efficiency of governance by achieving more influence with less costly governance arrangements.

Are there specific goals that are in conflict with each other? Is there a mechanism for resolving conflicts between stakeholders, for prioritizing goals, and for coordinating multiple simultaneous claims on the system? This set of questions addresses the possibility of governance that suffers because of the diversity of interests and goals within a multi-organizational system.

This structural analysis of external governance opens with a definition of terms for discussing governance arrangements and ends with an effort to ensure that those arrangements are reasonably aligned with goals the achievement of which governance is expected to protect. Organizations conducting the analysis may vary in terms of how far they choose to go down this road from understanding to structuring the governance of a system. Nevertheless, the structural analysis should end with an attempt to synthesize its findings and communicate recommendations to system-level decisionmakers. If significant gaps or overlaps in governance coverage are unveiled, the structural analysis may conclude with suggestions for adding new governance relationships or merging existing ones. On the other hand, if the governance arrangements are understandable and well aligned with goals, the recommendation might be to perform an implementation audit as described in Chapter Four.

Chapter Four

THE IMPLEMENTATION AUDIT OF EXTERNAL GOVERNANCE

OVERVIEW

This chapter sets forth guidelines for auditing the effectiveness of governance in practice. The implementation audit differs from the structural analysis described in Chapter Three in the following ways:

*   The structural analysis seeks to describe governance arrangements and align them with stakeholder goals, while the implementation audit seeks to assess effectiveness in the actual performance of governance.

*   The structural analysis provides a broad overview of a network of relationships; even when it focuses on specific stakeholders and governance relationships, it places those in a larger context by mapping other stakeholders and relationships. On the other hand, the implementation audit focuses more closely on the operational details of the relationships between selected providers and stakeholders.

*   The structural analysis depends on official documents prescribing governance arrangements and on interviews with key personnel familiar with any informal governance relationships. It may be performed by a relatively small staff without much participation from the various organizations involved in the system. On the other hand, the implementation audit requires more detailed evidence from organizations in the system showing how governance works in practice. As a result, it

requires more time, staff effort, and multi-organizational participation.

- The structural analysis may be done as a planning exercise without a subsequent implementation audit. However, an implementation audit requires a preliminary understanding of the system such as that provided by the structural analysis. This does not mean that a new structural analysis is a prerequisite to every implementation audit, but it suggests that a structural analysis should have been done at least once, recently enough to remain valid.

- While both the structural analysis and the implementation audit contribute to an understanding of how the system is governed, which may be useful to a number of participants in the system, the two tasks differ in terms of who can and should act on their findings. Recommendations resulting from a structural analysis address potential changes in the system structure from the point of view of a system-level authority. Recommendations resulting from an implementation audit address potential changes in the operational behavior of specific stakeholders, intermediaries, and perhaps even providers.

- The scope of the implementation audit may in some cases be more limited than the scope of the structural analysis, both because the implementation audit has a different purpose and because it would be more costly than the structural analysis to carry out over the same scope.

We suggest that system-level authorities or key stakeholders undertake an implementation audit if they have concerns about their governance capabilities and outcomes. However, in the absence of an actual audit, this chapter may still serve as a stimulus for planners seeking to identify criteria for effective governance and as a starting point for other assessments of governance practices. Here we delineate what we mean by *governance effectiveness*, present a guide for planning an audit of external governance, and follow with sample criteria for assessing effective performance and capacity.[1]

---

[1]The practices suggested in this chapter come from various sources, including literature on quality auditing (Russell, 2000); public-sector performance measurement (Halachmi, 1996); public-sector compliance monitoring (Light, 1993); and program

Defining the Assessment of Governance Effectiveness

Governance is closely associated with the concept of accountability, which has received considerable attention in the public management literature. Government scholar Paul Light has identified three distinct models of accountability: organizations may be held accountable for *compliance* with rules, effectiveness in *performance* of a mission, and *capacity building* for future performance (Light, 1993, p. 14). Here, we discuss the implementation audit in these terms, emphasizing the latter two in our approach. We focus on the *effectiveness* of governance in terms of the performance of the system with respect to mission-level goals and the goals of key stakeholders, and in terms of the capacity of the system to continue responding to evolving goals and changing conditions.

The implementation audit does not, however, directly measure or assess the *system*'s effectiveness in achieving its goals. That is a governance task, but it is not the same thing as assessing *governance* effectiveness. Indeed, one of the things this audit seeks is evidence that the system's performance and capacity are being measured, monitored, and assessed by the organizations involved in governance.

A system may be effective in terms of current goal outcomes and yet lack effective governance. The goal outcomes may be at risk as circumstances change, unless stakeholders can gain the governance capacity to ensure that current successes are sustained in the future. The goals themselves might change over time, in which case the system needs to be capable of responding to future guidance from stakeholders. Current system effectiveness is evidence, but not proof, of good governance.

On the other hand, a system may have strong governance and yet be unable to demonstrate that it is currently effective in achieving specific goal outcomes. One case is where a system with a history of ineffectiveness is engaged in new reforms; goal outcomes have not yet improved, but governance has already gained effectiveness in bringing about change. A second case is where an intrinsically irre-

---

evaluation (Rossi, Freeman, and Wright, 1993). These practices are adapted here for use in the assessment of governance.

solvable tension exists among different stakeholder goals (e.g., budget constraints in the goals of one stakeholder or conflicting interests among different stakeholders). Effective governance allows at least peaceful coexistence among stakeholders and, at best, some sort of optimizing equilibrium among goals. In each of these cases, the evidence of effective governance lies in the process itself, either a change process or a reconciliation/equilibration process, rather than in the achievement of specific goals. Developing and sustaining such processes may be considered among the goals of governance.

Our emphasis on effectiveness contrasts with *compliance* accountability, which focuses on whether an organization conforms in practice with established policies. Assessing such conformity is a valid and often necessary governance function, fitting within the concept of control in the taxonomy of governance functions we described in Chapter Three. When overemphasized, however, it can distract an organization from efforts to improve performance and capacity (Light, 1993; and Behn, 2001).

When applied to external governance in a multi-organizational system, compliance accountability implies a focus on the degree to which actual governance practices conform to the governance arrangements set by policy. However, with regard to governance of the domains of ET&D, formal policies tend to focus on accountability for inputs and processes rather than on accountability for outcomes (Gates et al., 2001, pp. 59–61); there is often latitude for a broad range of both effective and ineffective governance practices within the region of strict compliance. Furthermore, compliance with rules and regulations is already the target of much concern in government, as seen in the work of the Inspectors General and the General Accounting Office. Thus, stakeholder dissatisfaction with governance of ET&D is more likely to have resulted from poorly structured governance arrangements and weakly implemented governance functions within the bounds of existing policy, rather than from outright noncompliance with established policy.

Auditing governance in terms of compliance runs the risk of focusing on the wrong things. It also implies a threat of negative sanctions to participating organizations; this could lead to an adversarial relationship between providers and stakeholders, reducing rather than increasing the influence of stakeholders over the outcomes that matter to them. Therefore, unless there is a strong prior perception that noncompliance is a major cause of ineffective governance, we do not recommend that compliance auditing be part of the strategic governance review.

Our approach also contrasts with the idea of assessing governance *efficiency*, the net benefit to the system of maintaining these specific governance arrangements and practices after considering their direct and indirect costs. This is a formidable task. Organizations are likely to account for the direct costs of governance activities under many budget categories. Indirect costs of governance, including not only the reporting burden on member organizations but also any opportunities lost because of the demands of responding to governance, are even less likely to be measured. Estimating benefits implies quantifying the outcomes of governance, the marginal contribution that governance makes in the achievement of key goals versus what would have been achieved under less governance. Because cost and benefit numbers will be so difficult to obtain or to estimate precisely, a valid assessment of governance efficiency would be a major undertaking beyond the scope of this report.

PLANNING THE AUDIT

Conducting an audit can be a costly undertaking. It requires fieldwork to obtain operational data, placing a time burden not only on the auditing staff but also on the responding organizations. It may introduce stress in the relationship between the auditing organization and the organizations being asked to provide access to data and operations. In light of these costs, a successful and efficient audit requires careful planning. According to *The Quality Audit Handbook*, proper quality audits must follow a prescribed sequence:

> Quality Audits must be prepared for (planning ahead), performed (conducting the audit), have the results reported (let everyone know what was found), and then have the results responded to (feedback on what is going to happen next) from the organization that was audited. It is common to refer to these as phases of an audit: preparation phase, performance phase, report phase, and follow-up and closure phase. (Russell, 2000, p. xxvi)

In the preparation phase, decisions must be made about the purpose and scope of the audit, who is to conduct the audit, and how information is to be gathered.

The Purpose of the Audit

The purpose of a specific audit will depend on the context and concerns of the authority, stakeholder, or intermediary that initiates the audit. The goals of a governance audit might include:

- to provide a detailed understanding of how governance actually works in the system

- to provide feedback about how well the goals of the system and/or of specific stakeholders are being protected through governance

- to provide suggestions for how to improve the system's overall accountability and responsiveness

- to provide suggestions for how to improve the influence of specific stakeholders over the outcomes that matter to them.

In planning an actual audit, we suggest that the purpose be operationalized by asking what will be done with the information generated by the audit. If a deeper understanding of governance is generated, how will this contribute to strategic planning efforts over time? If deficiencies or opportunities are noted, who will have the ability and motivation to do anything about them? To what organizations in the system will the results of the audit be made available, and what kinds of changes will they be able and willing to make on the basis of this information? Answering these questions in advance requires some awareness of the system's context and history, including the organizational, economic, and regulatory constraints it may face in making changes. Addressing these issues, however, will help improve the efficiency of the audit and make it more effectively contribute to the system.

The Scope of the Audit

The audit's scope needs to be limited to obtain the most benefit for the cost. In addition, the scope must be clearly communicated to participants so that the audit can proceed efficiently. Defining the scope in advance will help prevent spending time and effort on irrelevant and unauthorized evaluations. It will also guide the distinction between internal and external governance. The scope should be defined with respect to the organizations included in the audit, and with respect to the domains of ET&D relevant to the purpose of the audit.

If a recent structural analysis has been conducted for the specific system being audited, the scope of that analysis provides an ideal starting point for delineating the audit. However, an audit may be more restricted in scope than a structural analysis, and a deliberate decision as to scope should be made each time an audit is conducted, as part of the specification of the audit.

Establishing the scope of the audit requires that the following questions be answered:

- At what level is the system of interest defined? The answer could be as large as the entire DoD system of ET&D, in which case the audit will be prohibitively costly unless it is strictly limited in domain and detail. It could be as small as a single provider and the stakeholders it serves, which would either keep the cost lower or allow a comprehensive look at many domains in great detail. In most cases, the audit will be targeted at a system defined somewhere between these extremes.

- What organizations or entities are to be explicitly included in the audit? The list should include the providers and the stakeholders that are specifically relevant to the auditing authority's purpose for this audit. This does not necessarily mean identifying all of the key stakeholders involved in governance, as was done in the mapping exercise of the structural analysis.

- What domains of ET&D are explicitly included in the audit? Again, this depends on the purpose of the authority initiating the audit; the focus may be on a single area such as finance, a set of related areas such as faculty and curriculum, or all aspects of ET&D. Answering this in advance will provide essential guidance in conducting the audit, and it will reassure respondents who might be concerned about participating in an open-ended audit process.

Selecting Criteria

The next step in the audit plan involves specifying the assessment criteria. Criteria are vital because they give a yardstick against which to measure the operational realities observed in the audit. Selecting criteria in advance protects against the temptation to evaluate governance subjectively and then write criteria that justify the result.[2] Writing criteria for good governance and presenting them to members of the system, long in advance of an audit or even in the absence of an audit, has the added benefit of communicating to participants what results are expected from a set of governance arrangements.

However, there is a fine line between writing criteria for evaluation and writing rules for compliance. One difference lies in the type of sanction implied; noncompliance with rules results in negative sanctions, while achieving high standards of performance and capacity evaluation should result in positive benefits for participants. Another related difference lies in precision. Rules are often strictly worded and result in either-or determinations; an organization is either in compliance or not, regardless of whether its performance is truly effective. Criteria, on the other hand, are flexible in application to specific situations and promote continuous improvement in performance rather than a pass-fail mentality.

Here we suggest three "criteria for criteria." To the greatest extent possible, they should be measurement based, mission driven, and outcome oriented.

---

[2]In the course of an audit, information may be uncovered that could lead to the generation of new criteria. However, an audit is justifiable not as a quest for emergent criteria, but as an assessment of findings against criteria agreed upon before the start of the audit. Suggestions for new criteria may be included in the recommendations of the audit for consideration in planning future audits.

- *Measurement-based* criteria make objective assessment possible. This means that they use some sort of scale, the points of which are identified in terms of observable phenomena. Even a two-point scale, like a true-false question, counts as a measurement if empirical data can be reliably mapped onto the two points. Attitudes and opinions can be measured with a variety of scales developed according to the methods of social science research.[3] What is essential is that criteria be based on observable distinctions.

- *Mission-driven* criteria direct an assessment toward the external purpose of the system; they could also be described as *demand driven*, especially in the case of workforce ET&D. It is natural for organizations to focus on supply rather than demand, on internal survival and growth needs rather than achievement of a mission assigned to them by an external authority.[4] In the public sector, and in the provision of ET&D for a large, multi-organizational system, it may be even easier to neglect demand. Providers may define their mission in terms of what they prefer to do and have been doing, rather than what the larger system and key stakeholders need them to do. Criteria for assessing the external governance of providers should emphasize a mission that is external to the providers.

- *Outcome-oriented* criteria focus on results rather than inputs and processes. In activities where outcomes are difficult to measure, as in much of government and in ET&D, it is tempting for organizations to focus on things that are more easily measured. This leads to a focus on such things as budget size, personnel qualifications, and enrollments, rather than on the achievements that matter for educational quality and that make a meaningful dif-

---

[3]Just as a ruler used to measure a physical object must be calibrated to generally recognized units of length, a scale used in measuring social phenomena should be validated so that there is general agreement about what the points mean. See Judd, Smith, and Kidder (1991, pp. 145–170) and Churchill (1995, pp. 451–489) for descriptions of scales commonly used in social science research.

[4]In a market economy, business firms receive their funds from the customers they serve, and they must be demand driven to thrive—or so it would seem. In fact, even the private sector faces the perennial problem of what marketing scholar Theodore Levitt calls "marketing myopia," the tendency of firms to be product oriented rather than demand oriented (i.e., to produce what they want to produce rather than what their customers want to buy) (Levitt, 1986, pp. 141–172).

ference to external stakeholders.[5] Governance criteria should emphasize outcomes wherever possible. In some cases, such as when assessing the capacity for ongoing governance, it is necessary to use process-oriented criteria simply because future outcomes cannot be observed. Such criteria should be justified by evidence that there is indeed a linkage between a process and the sort of outcome it is intended to generate.[6]

Later sections of this chapter discuss some possible criteria for assessing governance in general terms; more specific criteria should be written in operational terms that support the purpose of the audit in the context of the institutions and domains within its scope. Not all of the criteria we suggest will be relevant to a specific audit, and audit planners may conceive of criteria other than the ones described here.

Determining Who Will Conduct the Audit

The audit will be authorized by a system-level authority or key stakeholder, but it may be performed by an intermediary in a manner similar to a CPA firm conducting a financial audit. In compliance auditing, the persons conducting the audit are generally expected to have a degree of independence from the entity being audited. In an audit oriented toward performance and capacity, as emphasized here, the degree of independence required may be less, depending on the purpose of the audit.

The question arises whether an institution should be established with specific responsibility for conducting governance audits. In the case of compliance auditing, with a need for independence, this is an obvious and traditional approach. In the case of performance auditing, it is not so clear that this is the right approach. Robert Behn argues forcefully against designating specific institutions to conduct performance auditing in government (Behn, 2001, pp. 201–203). Such institutions naturally tend to define performance according to

---

[5]Gates et al. (2001) provides a more thorough discussion of outcome measurement as an approach to evaluating the quality of ET&D.

[6]There is a parallel between this criterion, that there should be a linkage between a process and its intended outcome, and the methodological criterion of validity, that there should be a linkage between a metric and the outcome it is intended to measure. See Gates et al. (2001) for a discussion of validity in measurement.

their own standards and then to audit compliance with those standards. What is needed in a multi-organizational system is multidirectional accountability for performance, obtaining feedback from a variety of institutions and taking into account the diversity of perspectives on what government performance means.

Behn's view is congruent with the concept of governance underlying this report, but assessing governance as such may be different from assessing organizational performance. A governance audit is more specialized than a performance evaluation and involves issues at a higher order of abstraction. Efficiency in conducting such audits may grow over time as an organization conducts more audits. Thus, in a system that needs repeated governance auditing, there may be a need for an institution to specialize in governance auditing.

However, this institution should not be a traditional auditing organization such as an Inspector General's office. A conscious effort is needed to avoid associating governance auditing with compliance accountability and an overreliance on procedures created by the auditing profession for verifying compliance. Perhaps an intermediary specializing in governance issues could become not only a designated institution for conducting nonadversarial governance audits but also an organizational resource for knowledge about governance and a facilitator for organizations wishing to perform self-audits.

Gathering Operational Information

In contrast to the structural analysis, which relies on policy documents and interviews with system-level administrators, the implementation audit requires data from the field, specifically from the providers and the stakeholders included in the scope of the audit. However, because the audit will not assess compliance with rules, there is no need to dig for hidden information in the manner of a financial audit. The audit assesses governance according to the criteria chosen earlier and thus involves gathering evidence as to how well the system fulfills these criteria. Auditors will obtain various forms of evidence about the history and day-to-day implementation of governance relationships among entities. Assessment then proceeds by considering the weight of the evidence relative to each criterion.

This approach is similar to the way many accrediting agencies review educational institutions. In the accreditation process, a school is typically asked to perform an analytical self-assessment according to criteria set by the agency and then to provide reviewers with evidence supporting this self-assessment. In this model, the accrediting agency's standards include descriptions of the types of evidence or indicators that would be considered to validate an assessment under each criterion.

Following this model, specific types of evidence should be named in the governance audit plan, and entities subject to the audit can then provide those items to the audit team. Site visits and personal interviews can be used to supplement—and if necessary verify—the documentary evidence. This approach provides enormous flexibility in making the audit appropriate to its purpose and context; it allows a cooperative rather than an adversarial relationship between auditors and respondents.

ASSESSING THE EFFECTIVENESS OF EXTERNAL GOVERNANCE

The purpose of external governance in a system of ET&D is to ensure that the network of providers fulfills the system's mission and achieves the goals of key stakeholders, particularly with respect to quality and productivity. An obvious approach to assessing the effectiveness of governance would be to measure whether the system's mission is being fulfilled and stakeholder goals are being achieved. The trouble with this approach is that *this is exactly what governance is supposed to be doing* (among other things). Assessing governance by repeating its evaluation of system performance is like checking a sum by adding it again. This approach may be cost-effective when counting change at the grocery, but it represents costly duplication of effort in a large multi-organizational system. Thus, the implementation audit will seek to measure how well goal fulfillment is being governed rather than how well goals are actually being fulfilled. Such an approach involves an assessment of governance performance, showing that the system is responsive to the influence of stakeholders, as well as governance capacity, showing that governance activities within the system promote responsiveness to the continuing influence of stakeholders over the long term.

We list four suggested criteria here and then discuss each in turn.

1. There is evidence that system outcomes are being defined, measured, and evaluated relative to goals.

2. There is evidence that providers, intermediaries, and key stakeholders are communicating frequently and transparently.

3. There is evidence that providers and intermediaries are responsive to key stakeholder guidance.

4. There is evidence that key stakeholders are being satisfied.

Criterion 1. There Is Evidence that System Outcomes Are Being Defined, Measured, and Evaluated Relative to Goals.

Monitoring and assessing system performance are critical governance functions, and they provide the information required for other governance functions such as planning and coordination. Financial measures of performance are nearly universal, and sophisticated but easy-to-use systems have been developed in that domain. However, performance measurement in terms of outcomes is a more complex task, yet it is often done with less sophisticated tools than are used for financial measurement, so it may be neglected (Anthony and Govindarajan, 1998; and Halachmi, 1996). Effective governance requires that outcomes be measured on an ongoing basis and evaluated relative to the mission, vision, and goals established for the system by system-level stakeholders in consultation with other key stakeholders. This criterion assumes a prior alignment of the system's mission, vision, and goals with key stakeholder goals, as described in Chapter Three. It also assumes that these system-level goals have been defined explicitly enough to be used as a basis for measuring outcomes.

It should be easy for auditors to obtain evidence that such measurement and evaluation are indeed taking place regularly; when done properly, the very process leaves a documentary trail and a body of historical data for future reference. In addition, auditors may seek evidence that there is good management of the data resulting from measurement. For example, are data captured at the source in a timely manner, or are they based on delayed and/or second-hand reports? Are databases maintained regularly, with procedures to identify and correct data errors? Does frequent feedback from database users contribute to corrections of the data and improvements in the system?

It may also be useful to assess the validity of evaluation processes and their conclusions, which will require expertise in program evaluation (Rossi, Freeman, and Wright, 1993). However, such expert assessments are optional in this review of governance. In systems without highly developed governance processes, significant progress may be realized simply by ensuring that the goal outcomes that matter are being regularly measured and evaluated on behalf of key stakeholders. Relevant evidence may include published policies and procedures for collecting data, including a specification of the input items to be reported; database reports produced regularly over a period of time, along with statistical analyses and management comments; and documents showing that the available data are used in evaluating outcomes.

Criterion 2. There Is Evidence that Providers, Intermediaries, and Key Stakeholders Are Communicating Frequently and Transparently.

Communication is a governance function that enables a multi-organizational system to work. Without frequent two-way communication, providers will not know what goals stakeholders expect to be met, and stakeholders will not know what efforts providers are making and what constraints providers face in meeting those goals. As representatives of other stakeholder interests, intermediaries also need to engage in such communication. Effective communication consists of more than formal guidance through directives and formal feedback through measurement of outcomes. The ideal is for participants to continually modify and verify their mutual understanding in real time.[7] This is challenging even in relatively simple contexts such as teamwork among a small number of individuals; it is even more

---

[7]Communication plays roles other than the transmission of formal information for control purposes; the symbolic meanings embedded in the very act of communication are important to the evolution and maintenance of organizational relationships (Overman and Loraine, 1994).

difficult in multi-organizational systems and requires a commitment to communication as a priority.

Transparency in communication means that relevant information is openly and immediately shared. Deficiencies in transparency may be intentional or unintentional. They may result from a number of causes, including a neglect of communication as a priority, a concern for protecting organizational control over information resources, a lack of adequate systems and organizational capacity, and perhaps a natural aversion to accountability. Transparency is lost not only when information is withheld, but also when it is distorted through improper processing or hidden in a confusing overload of disconnected details. Of course, some limits to inter-organizational transparency may be appropriate, especially in a national defense setting. However, the logic of governance requires that the system-level authority or key stakeholder agree to such limits.

Evidence of frequent and transparent communication may be obtained from published policies and procedures, including clearly identified descriptions of goals, copies of correspondence, and interviews with participants. In keeping with the audit strategy of letting organizations provide their own evidence, auditors do not need unlimited access to correspondence files; they can form an assessment of governance capacity based on the type, quantity, and quality of the particular records reviewed.

Criterion 3. There Is Evidence that Providers and Intermediaries Are Responsive to Key Stakeholder Guidance.

If there is good communication among organizations, the next question is whether such communication results in an effective mechanism for giving guidance that results in change. If governance is defined in terms of influence, then effective governance will be observable in the results of that influence. To address this criterion, auditors can seek evidence that stakeholders involved in governance have in fact succeeded in influencing the provision of ET&D within the domain of interest.

Some of the evidence submitted for Criterion 3 will be similar to the documentation supporting Criterion 2; it should show not only communication but also change taking place. Effective influence might take the form of corrective direction given by a stakeholder and accepted by a provider, resulting in measured improvements. Such cases will make auditing easy, because both parties should be able to produce documentary evidence such as letters, reports, and responses to reports showing the correction and resulting improvement.[8]

Other forms of influence might be more subtle and difficult—but not impossible—to measure. For example, an intermediary may assert that it has influenced ET&D by acting as a liaison to increase communication between providers and other stakeholders and by becoming a clearinghouse for information about educational quality. Evidence of this might be derived from records showing that increased communication and usage of information resources actually took place. Oral histories obtained through interviews with administrators may provide further evidence of governance influence.

Intermediaries should also be able to show evidence of their responsiveness to key stakeholder concerns. To a large extent, the work of governance is performed by intermediaries acting on behalf of key stakeholders. This is especially true in a multi-organizational system of ET&D, where governance of ET&D, while important, is not one of the highest priorities for many stakeholders. Multiple stakeholders may form explicit or implicit alliances in which they rely on the services of an intermediary to protect their mutual interests. In assessing governance capacity, the implementation audit seeks evidence that such intermediaries have in fact made changes based on input from the relevant stakeholders.

This audit takes a key stakeholder point of view and assumes that the various governing and advisory boards in a multi-organizational system of ET&D serve, along with accrediting agencies, as intermediaries to further the goals of identifiable stakeholders or system-level authorities. Given this assumption, the responsiveness of those in-

---

[8]A special case of this criterion may be found when a provider or intermediary is a formal component of the system, rather than a relatively independent vendor or association, and when the key stakeholder in question is a system-level stakeholder. In such a case, the audit may seek additional evidence that the mission, vision, and goals of the system component have been developed and updated through a strategic planning process in which the system-level stakeholder was engaged.

termediaries to key stakeholder concerns is a critical indicator of governance capacity.

Evidence relevant to this criterion might include minutes of board meetings, accrediting agency bylaws, and copies of correspondence between key stakeholders and the intermediaries of concern. Further assessment approaches could look at the composition of boards and accrediting commissions as well as their staffs and review teams. How qualified are these individuals to perform their governance roles? Is there evidence of conflicts of interest or resistance to appropriate stakeholder concerns? Is there a review process for evaluating the work of the intermediaries? Do key stakeholders have a role in the governance of the intermediary, such as having a voice in the selection of board members? Can members be replaced for cause? The implementation audit does not require a comprehensive assessment of governing boards and/or accrediting agencies, but the evidence obtained in a light review may reveal whether further examination is warranted.

Criterion 4. There Is Evidence that Key Stakeholders Are Being Satisfied.

The repeated theme of these criteria is that external governance exists to serve the goals of stakeholders, including a system-level authority defined as the stakeholder for the system's overall mission. It is not necessary for the audit team to identify and measure all of these goals; governance success can often be measured indirectly by measuring the satisfaction of stakeholders with their own goal outcomes. Stakeholder dissatisfaction constitutes strong evidence that governance is ineffective. On the other hand, stakeholder satisfaction alone does not demonstrate effective governance, but it contributes positive weight to the assessment of effectiveness in conjunction with other evidence produced by the audit.

Stakeholder satisfaction with goal outcomes is a measure of actual governance performance; to assess governance capacity, it may be useful to ask how satisfied stakeholders are with the *process* of governance. Satisfaction with outcomes does not by itself show that stakeholders view governance as contributing causally to those outcomes; goals may have been achieved in spite of poor governance and thus may be at risk. Furthermore, research in consumer behavior shows that the opportunity to voice concerns makes an important difference in satisfaction with a vendor relationship over time (Hirschman, 1970). This finding about individuals is echoed for organizations in transaction cost economics (Williamson, 1996). What matters most to a stakeholder may not be a single transaction or the fulfillment of a specific goal, but the maintenance of a long-term relationship in which the stakeholder can count on having a voice in the governance of future transactions and goals.

Satisfaction measurement is a well-established field of social science research with broad applications, including marketing, education, and political science. One of the most important insights of this research is that satisfaction is not strictly a matter of outcomes, but of correspondence between expectations and outcomes. Thus, while it may be difficult to measure precise outcomes relative to diverse goals, it is possible to measure the sense that stakeholders have of the distance between their expectations and their outcomes. Techniques for such measurement can be found in Zeithaml, Berry, and Parasuraman (1990), Dutka (1994), Hayes (1998), and other management and social science literature. The research design may focus on goal fulfillment and on specific dimensions of the governance process—such as transparent communication—and investigate the degree of stakeholder satisfaction with respect to each. This criterion in effect places the assessment of effectiveness in the hands of the stakeholders to whom it matters most.

REPORTING AND FOLLOW-UP

The audit is not finished once these assessments have been performed. A number of steps remain. The organizations involved in the audit need to be informed of preliminary findings and given an opportunity to respond. Recommendations and overall observations should be documented and disseminated to appropriate parties. The audit itself should also be documented for future reference and reviewed for lessons that will make future such audits more efficient and effective.

Responding to Preliminary Findings

The initial results of the audit need to be discussed with the participants, who should be given a chance to respond with corrections or clarifications. Auditors' observations and judgments are fallible, so it is vital to obtain feedback from those who are more familiar with the organizational context. This is true of financial audits and compliance audits; it is even more important for performance and capacity audits, where maintaining a positive relationship among organizations requires conducting the audit in a cooperative manner.

Generating Recommendations and Conclusions

The audit should generate specific recommendations for action and general conclusions for better understanding of governance in the system. The emphasis of these results will depend on the purpose of the audit. Ideally, the original directive authorizing the audit will contain a list of objectives to be reached, and the audit report will address each of these objectives with answers obtained from the audit. The recommendations are likely to be in the form of suggestions rather than strict instructions. Significant thought should be given to how the recommended changes can be brought about within the existing organizational context and constraints.

Aside from the original objectives, unanticipated results might arise during the course of the audit. Significant opportunities for improvement of governance, and significant deficiencies in the practice of governance, should be noted and communicated to the relevant authorities for addressing. There may also be insights that lead to revision of the criteria so that they more appropriately address the operational issues and information sources found in the field.

Implementation and Evaluation

In a compliance audit, the auditing authority expects the organization being audited to make corrective changes on the observed points of noncompliance; a follow-up correspondence ensures that these changes are made and noted. In this performance and capacity audit of governance, it might not be necessary for the audit team to verify that the recommended changes are adopted. However, the system-level authority or key stakeholder that initiated the audit will want to follow up with the organizations involved in the audit, tracking to what extent the recommendations are adopted. For maximum advantage, there should be an attempt to measure the effects of these changes to confirm that the changes made the expected difference in outcomes.

Reviewing the Audit

Finally, the audit should be reviewed for lessons applicable to future audits. Auditors may make notes regarding the methods used, obstacles encountered, and issues raised during the course of the audit. Perhaps most important, feedback from the responding organizations about the audit experience will help future planners and auditors maintain positive relationships and do a more efficient job of collecting information.

Chapter Five

RECOMMENDATIONS AND CONCLUSIONS

This report describes a strategic governance review, a two-pronged approach to examining external governance within a multi-organizational system of ET&D. The goal of this governance review is to enable key system-level authorities and stakeholders to obtain better outcomes and higher responsiveness from the organizations that serve their needs.

On the basis of this study, we make the following recommendations for the Chancellor's office, the DoD system of ET&D, and more generally any other multi-organizational system that might find these tools useful.

Advocate and Facilitate System-Level and Demand-Side Governance on the Part of Key Stakeholders within the System.

Effective governance of the components of a multi-organizational system can be critical to the successful strategic management of the system. A hands-off, decentralized, and indirect approach to governance of the system is appropriate in many cases, but even this implies a strategic planning choice that should be reviewed and evaluated on occasion. If there are system-level stakeholders, there should be a system-level approach to governance. But a system-level governance strategy does not necessarily imply centralized control.

A system of ET&D that cuts across the hierarchical boundaries of organizations with primary missions other than ET&D is likely to include multiple stakeholders, including demand-side stakeholders—

the employers seeking to obtain a trained workforce—who could benefit from reviewing and improving their own governance over the elements of the system. However, these stakeholders may be limited by a lack of capacity for governance and/or by a lack of institutional clarity about the appropriateness of such governance efforts within a system traditionally perceived as hierarchical. A system-level strategic review of governance can empower key stakeholders to exercise more effective governance in pursuit of their own goals.

Encourage All Key Stakeholders to Undertake a *Structural Analysis* of Governance as Part of Their Own Strategic Planning Function.

The first half of the strategic governance review, which involves describing governance arrangements and aligning them with goals, should become a standard element of strategic planning for key stakeholders in a multi-organizational system (e.g., the functional sponsors, or more precisely the offices responsible for ET&D within the functional sponsors' organizations), and for system-level intermediaries charged with contributing to the overall mission of the system (e.g., the Chancellor's office with respect to DoD ET&D). This task does not need to be done frequently, but there are likely to be major benefits from doing it at least once, with occasional revisits as the system's circumstances change.

Engage in System-Specific Development and Pilot Testing before Performing an *Implementation Audit* of Governance.

The second half of the strategic governance review described in this report is intended to be suggestive of the kind of audit that could be done by a key stakeholder. However, it is not a formally tested model ready for adoption. Before such an audit is undertaken, it is important that an audit plan based on the specific circumstances and goals of the system in question be written. Once such a plan is created, it should be conducted on a small scale to obtain feedback and operational experience that can be incorporated into the design of the audit before it is performed on a wide scale.

Perform *Implementation Audits* on a Case-by-Case Basis for Major Subsystems or Key Stakeholders (e.g., Functional Sponsors) That Have Salient Problems with Responsiveness and Effectiveness.

Auditing the implementation of governance is likely to be costly, both to the auditing entity and to the organizations being audited. It also runs the danger of becoming yet another layer of permanent bureaucracy, increasing the reporting burden of organizations and institutionalizing an excessively compliance-oriented culture. While auditing financial practices and operational results is a valuable part of first-level governance, auditing governance implementation is a second-level governance task that should not dominate institutional priorities except in response to perceived shortcomings. When a major subsystem seems to be unresponsive to key stakeholder concerns, or when a key stakeholder seems to encounter obstacles to governance rather than responsive cooperation, an implementation audit may be warranted.

Establish a Center for the Development and Retention of Governance Knowledge and Evaluation Capacity.

Unlike accounting, governance is not something with a body of generally accepted principles and a corps of equivalently trained professionals. Governance tends to be adapted over time to the history and needs of a specific system and cannot be re-created at will according to a universal model. Thus, a multi-organizational system can benefit from having an office that develops and shares governance concepts and tools with the system's stakeholders. Such an office can advocate the strategic review of governance and provide resources that empower stakeholders to review and improve their own governance. In the case of DoD, such a function might well be performed by the Chancellor's office. However, because of the negative or threatening implications of governance *auditing*, we do not recommend that the Chancellor's office actually perform the implementation audit; such a role might dilute its efforts to advocate quality and productivity among the providers of ET&D. On the other hand, the Chancellor's office is well positioned to perform a system-level *structural analysis* of governance and to support functional sponsors and other system-level stakeholders when and if they choose to conduct implementation audits.

BIBLIOGRAPHY

Ackoff, R. L., *Creating the Corporate Future*, New York: John Wiley & Sons, 1981.

Alter, Catherine, and Jerald Hage, *Organizations Working Together*, Thousand Oaks, Calif.: Sage Publications, 1993.

Anthony, Robert N., and Vijay Govindarajan, *Management Control Systems*, 9th ed., Boston, Mass.: Irwin McGraw-Hill, 1998.

Augustine, Catherine H., Dina G. Levy, Roger Benjamin, Tora K. Bikson, Glenn A. Daley, Susan M. Gates, Tessa Kaganoff, and Joy S. Moini, *Strategic Assessment and Development of Interorganizational Influence in the Absence of Hierarchical Authority*, Santa Monica, Calif.: RAND, MR-1561-OSD, 2002.

Behn, Robert D., *Rethinking Democratic Accountability*, Washington, D.C.: Brookings Institution Press, 2001.

Box, Richard C., Gary S. Marshall, B. J. Reed, and Christine M. Reed, "New Public Management and Substantive Democracy," *Public Administration Review*, Vol. 61, No. 5, September/October 2001, pp. 608–619.

Chavis, David M., Paul Florin, and Michael Felix, "Nurturing Grassroots Initiatives for Community Development: The Role of Enabling Systems," in T. Mizrahi and J. Morrison, eds., *Community Organization and Social Administration: Advances, Trends and Emerging Principles*, New York: The Haworth Press, 1993.

Chisholm, Donald, *Coordination Without Hierarchy: Informal Structures in Multiorganizational Systems*, Berkeley, Calif.: University of California Press, 1989.

Churchill, Gilbert A., Jr., *Marketing Research: Methodological Foundations*, 6th ed., Fort Worth, Tex.: The Dryden Press, 1995.

Deavers, Kenneth L., Max R. Lyons, and Anita U. Hattiangadi, *A Century of Progress, A Century of Change: The American Workplace 1999*, Washington, D.C.: Employment Policy Foundation, 1999.

Dutka, Alan F., *AMA (American Marketing Association) Handbook for Customer Satisfaction: A Complete Guide to Research, Planning & Implementation*, Lincolnwood, Ill.: NTC Business Books, 1994.

Freeman, R. E., *Strategic Management: A Stakeholder Approach*, Marshfield, Mass.: Pitman Publishing, 1984.

French, J. R. P., Jr., and B. Raven, "The Bases of Social Power," in D. Cartwright, ed., *Studies in Social Power*, Ann Arbor, Mich.: Institute for Social Research, 1959, pp.150–167.

Gates, Susan M., Catherine H. Augustine, Roger Benjamin, Tora K. Bikson, Eric Derghazarian, Tessa Kaganoff, Dina G. Levy, Joy S. Moini, and Ron W. Zimmer, *Ensuring the Quality and Productivity of Education and Professional Development Activities: A Review of Approaches and Lessons for DoD*, Santa Monica, Calif.: RAND, MR-1257-OSD, 2001.

Gill, Brian P., *The Governance of the City University of New York: A System at Odds with Itself*, Santa Monica, Calif.: RAND, MR-1141-EDU, 2000.

Hage, Jerald, and Catherine Alter, "Interorganizational Network Systems: A New Institution and Governance Mechanism," in Richard M. Coughlin, ed., *Morality, Rationality, and Efficiency: Studies in Socio-Economics*, Armonk, N.Y: M. E. Sharpe, Inc., 1991, pp. 265–285.

Halachmi, Arie, ed., *Organizational Performance and Measurement in the Public Sector: Toward Service, Effort and Accomplishment Reporting*, Westport, Conn.: Quorum Books, 1996.

Hayes, Bob E., *Measuring Customer Satisfaction: Survey Design, Use, and Statistical Analysis Methods, 2nd ed.*, Milwaukee, Wisc.: American Society for Quality, 1998.

Hirschman, Albert O., *Exit, Voice and Loyalty: Responses to Decline in Firms, Organizations, and State*s, Cambridge, Mass.: Harvard University Press, 1970.

Hynes, Michael, Sheila Nataraj Kirby, and Jennifer Sloan, *A Casebook of Alternative Governance Structures and Organizational Forms*, Santa Monica, Calif.: RAND, MR-1103-OSD, 2000.

Jones, Candace, William S. Hesterly, and Stephen P. Borgatti, "A General Theory of Network Governance: Exchange Conditions and Social Mechanisms," *Academy of Management Review*, Vol. 22, No. 4, 1997, pp. 911–945.

Judd, Charles M., Eliot R. Smith, and Louise H. Kidder, *Research Methods in Social Relations*, 6th ed., Fort Worth, Tex.: Harcourt Brace Jovanovich College Publishers, 1991.

Kearns, Kevin P., "The Strategic Management of Accountability in Nonprofit Organizations: An Analytical Framework," *Public Administration Review*, Vol. 54, No. 2, 1994, pp. 185–192.

Levitt, Theodore, *The Marketing Imagination*, expanded ed., New York: The Free Press, 1986.

Levy, Dina G., Roger Benjamin, Tora Kay Bikson, Eric Derghazarian, James A. Dewar, Susan M. Gates, Tessa Kaganoff, Joy S. Moini, Thomas S. Szayna, and Ron W. Zimmer, *Strategic and Performance Planning for the Office of the Chancellor for Education and Professional Development in the Department of Defense*, Santa Monica, Calif.: RAND, MR-1234-OSD, 2001a.

Levy, Dina G., Harry Thie, Albert A. Robbert, Scott Naftel, Charles Cannon, Rudolph H. Ehrenberg, and Matthew Gershwin, *Characterizing the Future Defense Workforce*, Santa Monica, Calif.: RAND, MR-1304-OSD, 2001b.

Light, Paul C., *Monitoring Government: Inspectors General and the Search for Accountability*, Washington, D.C.: Brookings Institution Press, 1993.

Light, Paul C., *The Tides of Reform: Making Government Work, 1945–1995*, New Haven, Conn.: Yale University Press, 1997.

Light, Paul C., *The New Public Service*, Washington, D.C.: Brookings Institution Press, 1999.

Management Sciences for Health and United Nations Children's Fund, *The Guide to Managing for Quality*, available at http://erc.msh.org/quality, 1998.

Mitchell, R., B. Agle, and D. Wood, "Towards a Theory of Stakeholder Identification and Salience: Defining the Principle of Who and What Really Counts," *Academy of Management Review*, Vol. 22, No. 4, 1997, pp. 853–886.

Moe, Ronald C., "The Emerging Federal Quasi Government: Issues of Management and Accountability," *Public Administration Review*, Vol. 61, No. 3, 2001, pp. 290–312.

Moe, Terry M., "Toward a Theory of Public Bureaucracy," in Oliver E. Williamson, ed., *Organization Theory: From Chester Barnard to the Present and Beyond*, expanded ed., New York: Oxford University Press, 1995, pp. 116–153.

Office of the Assistant Secretary of Defense for Force Management Policy, *Management Reform Memorandum 3: Streamlining the Management of Educational and Professional Development Programs*, December 1997.

Oudman, Ruud, Arjen M. Vos, and Jeroen Biesboer, *Stakeholder Analysis: A Review*, available at http://panoramix.univ-paris1.fr/CRINFO/dmrg/MEE98/misop001/index.html, 1998.

Overman, Sam E., and Donna T. Loraine, "Information for Control: Another Management Proverb?" *Public Administration Review*, Vol. 54, No. 2, 1994, pp. 193–196.

Overseas Development Administration, *Guidance Note on How to Do Stakeholder Analysis of Aid Projects and Programmes*, available at http://www.euforic.org/gb/stake1.htm, 1995.

Pfeffer, Jeffrey, and Gerald R. Salancik, *The External Control of Organizations: A Resource Dependence Perspective*, New York: Harper & Row, 1978.

Rossi, Peter H., Howard E. Freeman, and Sonia R. Wright, *Evaluation: A Systematic Approach*, 5th ed., Thousand Oaks, Calif.: Sage Publications, 1993.

Russell, J. P., ed., *The Quality Audit Handbook*, 2nd ed., Milwaukee, Wisc.: ASQ Quality Press, 2000.

Savage, Grant T., Rosemary L. Taylor, Timothy M. Rotarius, and John A. Buesseler, "Governance of Integrated Delivery Systems/ Networks: A Stakeholder Approach," *Health Care Management Review*, Vol. 22, No. 1 , 1997, pp. 7–20.

Scholl, Hans J., "Applying Stakeholder Theory to E-Government: Benefits and Limits," available at http://www.albany.edu/~hjscholl/Scholl_IFIP_2001.pdf, 2002.

Senge, Peter M., *The Fifth Discipline: The Art and Practice of the Learning Organization*, New York: Doubleday, 1990.

Tirole, Jean, "Corporate Governance," *Econometrica*, Vol. 69, No. 1, 2001, pp. 1–36.

Van Raak, Arno, and Aggie Paulus, "A Sociological Systems Theory of Interorganizational Network Development in Health and Social Care," *Systems Research and Behavioral Science*, Vol. 18, 2001, pp. 207–224.

Van Wart, Montgomery, "The First Step in the Reinvention Process: Assessment," *Public Administration Review*, Vol. 55, No. 5, (September/October) 1955, pp. 429–438.

Weiss, Carol H., *Evaluation Research: Methods of Assessing Program Effectiveness*, Englewood Cliffs, N.J.: Prentice-Hall, 1972.

Wiig, Karl M., "Knowledge Management: An Introduction and Perspective," *The Journal of Knowledge Management*, Vol. 1, No. 1 1997, pp. 6–14.

Williamson, Oliver E., *The Economic Institutions of Capitalism*, New York: The Free Press, 1985.

Williamson, Oliver E., *The Mechanisms of Governance*, New York: Oxford University Press, 1996.

Wilson, James Q., *Bureaucracy: What Government Agencies Do and Why They Do It*, New York: Basic Books, 1989.

Zeithaml, V. A., L. L. Berry, and A. Parasuraman, *Delivering Quality Service: Balancing Customer Perceptions and Expectations*, New York: The Free Press, 1990.